CONCILIUM

Religion in the Seventies

CONCILIUM

THE CRISIS
OF RELIGIOUS LANGUAGE

Edited by
Johann Baptist Metz and
Jean-Pierre Jossua

Herder and Herder

1973
HERDER AND HERDER NEW YORK
815 Second Avenue
New York 10017

ISBN: 0–8164–2541–8

Cum approbatione Ecclesiastica

Library of Congress Catalog Card Number: 72–12423

Printed in the United States

CONTENTS

PART II
BULLETIN

PART I
ARTICLES

Andrés Tornos

Symptoms and Causes of the Present Crisis in Religious Language

I. INTRODUCTION

1. *Two Ways of Seeing the Crisis*

THE anxiety felt by many Christians when they use or hear religious language has been called a crisis. Examples of this crisis are when we hear pious phrases unrelated to our daily lives, when, in the presence of great injustice or the absurdity of illness or death, words are spoken which do not match the gravity of the situation and perhaps especially when we can find no words at all to pray with our friends.

The word crisis as used in medicine can profitably be applied to the language of religion. When a doctor says that a sick person has reached a crisis or a critical point, he means that his illness has arrived at a point in the process of its development after which the patient will get better or worse. After this crisis, in other words, the situation is bound to change. In the context of religious language, then, the word crisis can mean a decisive point in the development of that language. To be able to discuss language at all, we must see it as if it were an illness, that is, as a developing process which follows certain laws and contains certain critical or decisive points or periods. The signs or symptoms of these periods as well as their hidden causes can, with experience, be recognized.

2. *Stating the Question*

Used in this sense, the word crisis can be applied to the evolution of religious language so long as we have a sufficiently clear theoretical understanding of linguistic development. Although several fairly firm conclusions have, however, been reached in the study of linguistic structures, what we know most clearly about the historical evolution or development of language is how much we do not know. Perhaps this is why the study of language has, in many places, been almost exclusively confined to structural linguistics. Scholars have tried to make it a scientific discipline even at the cost of ignoring all its psychological, sociological and historical aspects. I shall use the term crisis here in connection with the social process of language and its historical interpretation.

I am well aware of the difficulties and shall attempt to solve only a few of them. In the first place, I shall try to throw light on the historical process or development of religious language. Secondly, I shall discuss its critical stages and the present discontents as a critical situation. Finally, I shall try to find the real causes underlying the many symptoms.

II. Religious Language as Part of a Process

1. Formal Conditions for the Use of Language

In order to avoid confusion, it is important to distinguish four factors which are active in language—meaning, what is meant, sense and total interaction between persons or praxis.

(a) The meaning of the words we use depends on the total structure of the language with its grammar and vocabulary. It does not point primarily to the facts denoted by words, but rather to these words as connotation and to their relationships with other words in the world of ideas.

(b) I call what is meant the facts apprehended or experienced, or perhaps other objective realities, which we presume are the objects of the meaning expressed by words. We say that these are the realities denoted by language.

(c) By sense I mean the flavour of these words and facts, that is to say, the value attributed to what is said or heard, in the way what is meant is interrelated. Thus there can be no sense in someone talking about honour, even though he knows what it means.

(d) I use the word praxis for interpersonal relationships and actions in the context of language, in its sense, meaning and what is meant. I believe that this praxis is caused by very deep needs and that it has an historical structure.

With the help of these definitions, we can lay down the following conditions as a general law for the functioning of language:

(a) The verbal communication of what is meant is not independent of the structured interrelationships of praxis,

(b) because praxis determines whether such a communication makes sense or nonsense.

(c) The sense given to what is spoken results in the use, avoidance and occasionally the deformation of meanings.

(d) It is only through the strength of an adequate system of meanings, which is what languages usually are, that there can be a verbal interchange of what is meant which makes human praxis possible.

Thus these conditions are both mobile and circular. They are circular because what is meant conditions praxis, praxis conditions sense and sense conditions usage, and thus by and large meanings condition the interchange of what is meant. It is mobile because people and their praxis change and this changes the whole circle.

2. Momentary Usage and the Chain of Process

An example, the phrase "the love of Jesus Christ", will clarify this point. The real experiences meant by the expression, supposing that they exist, are the life of an individual person. But when these are communicated verbally to make positions clear and define purposes, they are the interaction of these experiences with those of other people. In this sense, the verbal interchange of what is meant conditions praxis.

And in its turn, praxis conditions the sense given to the words. When the "love of Jesus Christ" is invoked in an authoritarian way or is detached from the faithfulness to be expected between friends or is not sincere, for example, then the expression acquires a disturbing sense. But if it is used in a context of sincerity of faithfulness, then it has a positive sense. If it is used in both contexts, then it has an ambiguous sense.

These various senses determine the use of the phrase. A church leader or a militant Christian may cease to use the phrase if, in his environment, it has become disturbing, because then he will run the risk of being misunderstood. But if the phrase has acquired a positive sense, then he will tend to use it more than is necessary. Thus the sense felt in the words will decide when it is used.

Meaning is also determined by the use of the word. And, in fact, ceasing to use or misusing the expression "the love of Jesus Christ" makes it mean something no longer real or valid, but ambiguous. One has to explain how the phrase is intended to be understood or it either becomes an empty phrase or is given a remote or archaic meaning, or even becomes a fashionable paradox which connotes something other than its apparent meaning, even perhaps its opposite.

Finally, the alteration of meanings determines the group interchange of what is meant. It is, after all, difficult to express verbally a love of Jesus Christ if the words themselves have come to mean something else or if the experience is not sublime, but the words have come to sound sublime.

This explains the heading of this sub-section. The present or momentary use of the words "love of Jesus Christ" by us depends on the previous use of these words—we were taught them. It also depends on a complicated sociological and psychological process which brings the words to our mind and lips. The use of the words determines how our words strike other people, what they connote and denote for them (the meanings they contain and what is meant that is communicated by them). What is more, how the religious words we use strike others has repercussions upon us, qualifying our experience of what we say and the words we use to say it.

Thus we can speak of a chain of momentary uses of religious expressions in the constant social event of human communication. This chain takes words out of our control. We cannot make them be what we want or what we think they should logically be. Words, like certain books in medieval libraries, are chained. Their availability outside precise social contexts of meaning, what is meant, and sense is illusory. They do not tell others what they might be supposed to tell and perhaps cannot even tell us ourselves without deception.

It is true that words appear to be available in the most marvellous and delicate way, but this is for the particular moment. One might think one could speak of the love of Jesus Christ whenever one wanted. But to speak these words with our lips does not always give what is meant to others, still less does it give them our exact sense. Even by subjecting the words to a so-called meta-linguistic analysis, we may not succeed in relating them to other words in such a way as to make their meaning plain.

This is what I mean by the linguistic chain of process. I think it is essential to realize that the words are used within a process. Otherwise we cannot begin to understand what is meant by saying that our language is in a state of crisis. Then we must see how this process can have points of change, which can be discerned by their symptoms and interpreted by their causes. This is what I now propose to do.

III. Critical Stages in Religious Language

As the critical stages are the points of change, it is important to identify them in the historical process of language. This process, as we have said, can be interpreted at four levels:

(a) the interchange of human activities or praxis;

(b) language communicates what is meant;

(c) thus the language system, with its meanings, is shared by those who speak it and denotes approximately what the speaker wishes to denote;

(d) this results in social and individual satisfactions, which give the experience of sense to human activity and speech itself.

The independence of these four levels causes words to come and go, without constituting a crisis in language. This is because the linguistic structure allows for the coming and going of elements without damaging the system itself. This is a normal evolution of language which is different from a change in the actual system and the total conjunction of relationships of meaning. Then all religious speech might be threatened with change in what it meant and in its sense and moving towards something radically new. I shall now apply my four levels to an attempt to describe a critical situation, in which six stages can be distinguished.

1. In an undisturbed use of language, there can be mutations of praxis causing displacements in motivation and sense in the interchange of opinions about religious questions. Examples of this are the Reformation or the period following the Spanish Civil War in 1936.

2. The new senses and their accompanying values determine new meanings and alter, even if they do not break up, the grammar of the language as used in common speech.

3. They also produce new combinations of meaning and what is meant. The designative power of certain words becomes restricted to denote what is meant in a more highly particularized way, and thus their connotative power is weakened, as Marcuse observes,[1] in which case what is meant becomes cut off from the language like linguistic orphans, because they have been robbed of their birthright, that name by which they could be expressed. Suppose, for example, that the word "humility" becomes restricted to a purely servile attitude. Then the experience of a proper humility is cut off from the language and cannot be expressed.

4. This has three consequences:

(a) Because the word which has changed its meaning is not an arbitrary sound, but a term with its own place in the total system of linguistic terms, and because this place is not filled by new words since these are associated with what is usually meant and is now seeking a name, this cutting off of what is meant has repercussions on the total structure of meanings in the language. (For example, the classical virtues can no longer stand as the opposites of the vices.)

(b) The semantic alteration mentioned above (see stage 3) also alters the human interchange of praxis. Because experiences which have lost their name fall out of circulation, while the new highly particularized words are circulating fully, human discourse cannot be the same.

[1] *One-Dimensional Man* (London and Boston, 1964), chap. 4.

(c) The senses also change, because the experience of sense goes together with the interchange of praxis. Because what is meant has been cut off, the sense given to this is also cut off and makes its absence felt. (For example, uneducated people who made sense of their life by means of what is meant by "humility" can no longer do this.)

We should note here that the semantic changes described above in stage 3 have repercussions in stage 4 on all the factors of language. There are, however, three differences. The repercussion on the system of meanings is much slower than that on praxis and sense, is not so disturbingly present to experience and takes place in that special world of the structure of speech, which does not breathe, desire or suffer but is simply "there". The change in sense, on the other hand, is felt in the blood and causes numerous reactions in praxis, for example of those people who cannot make sense of their lives.

5. Changes in sense and praxis result in an anxious search for what is meant. The changes mentioned in stage 3 above continue to increase and have repercussions in all the ways mentioned in stage 4, so that, with each reinforcing the other, the whole language system changes and is threatened with destruction.

6. Small closed groups are sometimes unable to understand one another and the group breaks up. Sometimes the group interchange of what is meant is re-established through the structural transformation of the language of the group. A new praxis, the search for sense and the rediscovery of what is meant arise, together with a new world of meanings. In this schema of six aspects, the critical period is reached at the fifth stage, because the disruption of what is meant described in stage 3 is normal, although it may be unnoticed, in the constant process of renewal in any language. The resulting changes in meaning, sense and praxis mentioned in stage 4 can occur without structural change when they are understood and reorganized coherently by close-knit groups. But when this reorganization does not happen, they flood back in disorder on the semantic field and make it unusable.

If we say that the present situation of religious language is a state of crisis, this would mean that it satisfies the conditions for stage 5. There would have to be a general reaction against the nonsenses of life, a confused interaction between Christians, and a search for what is meant in religion. This would be found to be in a bad way, sometimes orphaned without name or idea, sometimes rigid and strictly over-particularized through the terrorism of an ardent party struggle.

In this study I am not prepared to say whether we have reached this situation or not. But I do want to try to distinguish the symptoms and the causes of such a crisis, if it exists.

IV. SYMPTOMS AND CAUSES OF THE CRISIS

The above attempt to clarify the linguistic process makes it possible for us to be brief here. From now on we will treat the words "symptom", "cause" and "crisis", which are medical metaphors, with some caution.

A symptom can be observed and used in diagnosing the linguistic process, but would not of itself have power to alter it. A cause of the crisis is what really produces the crisis, even though it may not be immediately apparent. According to our analysis, changes in praxis occur first. If they are not coped with effectively, they cause displacements in sense. These further occasion distortions in meaning and in what is meant.

They could be regarded more as symptoms because they can be observed and because they make us feel the difficulty of expressing ourselves in religious matters, because our language demands so many adjustments and new words, because it has been so broken up and because some religious experiences now have no name and others appear to have a name without definite connections with the rest of religious language. To fight this would be to try to cure a sickness by suppressing its symptoms.

It would be useful to spend time describing these phenomena and the point at which they begin to be symptomatic, if this could escape the danger of excessive speculation. As things are, I think it is more realistic to consider what are the changes in our praxis and how they work on our language. In this, we have to consider six points as possible sources of change, but we should not forget that Christian communities may fail to face up to them.

Firstly, technical and demographic changes have resulted in new forms of human work and relations. This new situation has modified the self-image of millions of men and women. Former roles are now not accepted and the new roles are confused. This is the second point.

Thirdly, the thematization of new political, technical and scientific meanings has summed up certain experiences of what is meant, such as oppression, consumption and operation, and this has an effect on our lives.

There are new means of communication with new possibilities and greater opportunities for interaction. We are in varied, subtle and often unaccustomed relationships with a great number of people. Our image of our fellow men in general is becoming totally different, almost without our noticing, and this changes our self-image. The praxis of interaction is thus given an unexpected impetus. The changes do not take place only at the individual level. There are also new forms of interaction between groups. Among Christian groups there has been an enormous change in the interaction between the different churches, and between them and the non-Christian religions or the doyens of culture, political action and intellectual criticism.

Hence the individual is much less aware than he imagines of what he represents to others. He does not usually realize this explicitly, but often has the feeling that he is walking on air and not on the ground of authentic relationships. The experience of personal identity will thus be profoundly disturbed[2] and this disturbance, which can even lead to the loss of personal or group identity altogether, is the ultimate source of change in praxis I am talking about. It has an immediate effect on the relationship between changes in praxis and language and causes a displacement and a cutting-off of sense. If one feels profoundly that one does not know what others take one for, it is very hard to express a sense which will give and receive certain messages. One then tends to use many highly particularized words and this results, as I have already said, in a crisis in the structures of connotation and meaning which are the heart of language.

[2] E. H. Erikson, *Identity, Youth and Crisis* (New York, 1968).

V. CONCLUSION

I have only been able to approach my subject in summary fashion; of course it could be greatly expanded. I have hardly said anything definite about the crisis in our own language. Defining such a crisis as a point of change in a process says nothing, if we do not say what this process is.

But this forms part of the very language difficulty I am discussing. How can we describe the process of Christian language? Can we use certain words to communicate what is meant when this may have altered? Does this mean using words which have become particularized?

There is no conclusive study on the real function of Christian language. This is not strange when there are no widely accepted theories on the function of language in general.[3] There is Ebeling's seductive hypothesis that the general function of language is to keep the future and freedom alive,[4] but for psychologists and sociologists this hypothesis is too ideological. I think, too, that it is particularly dangerous for theologians.

However, there are many questions about the future which are peculiarly ripe for linguistic interchange. Perhaps it is only in this way that the individual will be able to come to a growing organization of his internal and external stimuli, a clarification of his inter-personal relationships and a constant reconstruction of the necessary minimum of solidarity. The movement of language revolves round these possibilities on the way to freedom and the future.

At the religious and eschatological level, we can finally construct, by means of our schema used throughout this article, a model for interpreting the crisis, whose causes and systems we have been trying to diagnose.

Translated by Dinah Livingstone

---

[3] Jakobson's theory, which uses Shannon's work, is highly regarded and not just by specialist linguists, but never with great conviction. Cf. Miller and McNeill, "Psycholinguistics", in *Handbook of Social Psychology*, ed. Lindzey and Aronson, vol. 3 (Reading, Mass., 1969), pp. 751-4; see also H. Lefebvre, *Le Langage et la Société* (Paris, 1967).

[4] *Gott und Wort* (Tübingen, 1966), p. 44.

Danièle Hervieu-Léger

The Crisis in Doctrinal and Kerygmatic Language

I

THE Christian kerygma has always been a stumbling block or scandal. The Acts of the Apostles testifies to this—it begins with a direct confrontation between an ordered and relatively stable religious culture and the gospel message, the strangeness of which was attributed to the madness of those who proclaimed it. More directly it was attributed to drunkenness: "They are filled with new wine" (Acts 2. 13). The preaching of the cross forced a rift in Jewish culture and indeed in the culture of the ancient world as a whole. The evidence for this rift is nothing more nor less than the witness of the first Apostles. No purely human experience can verify or disprove it and it is precisely this which makes Paul describe the gospel as "a folly to Gentiles" (1 Cor. 1. 21).

But the kerygma has to be communicated verbally—it needs speech as its vehicle even if the speech is at odds with contemporary culture. Its "strangeness" is set against the backcloth of a culture which it at once transforms but upon which it is also dependent. As the kerygma is conveyed by means of a particular culture we may also describe it as what Paul Ricoeur has called what is available to be believed by a given period. It uses as its vehicle an "eschatological cosmology", that is a cosmology which employs the imagery of heaven and hell and portrays the world as a structure of religions in which the destiny of man is unfolded. But, to quote Ricoeur again, "this mythological framework was not in itself a scandal to the people of that time", although it has

19

become a scandal for modern man. For "it is not the cross which is the scandal (as it should be) but the means through which the message of the cross is communicated".[1] In the search for what is available to us to be believed, we are aware of how far removed we are from the world of the mythology in which the gospel was first preached. This should make us reflect very deeply about the language we use today, in a world where we are torn between a refusal to merely repeat the language of a by-gone culture and our inability to find a new language for ourselves. We cannot just write this off as a linguistic problem, as if the only thing we had to do was to translate and adapt the written texts. This is the mistake of so many pastors and scholars today. As the rural setting of the New Testament seems to mean so little to contemporary urban man, why not, they say, translate the message into a contemporary idiom by using the imagery and language of our technical and industrial society. This is a very real question. Would such a process involve reducing the gospel message in any way? Why do we not work towards a modern translation of the Bible—a translation using language familiar to all and using parables drawn from modern life and addressing itself to the facts of life as we know them today?

There can be no question, however, that the duty of the Christian preacher is to present the Christian faith in terms of the experience of his audience but this in itself also poses serious questions. We may well talk of the incongruity of biblical imagery and language but what this incongruity really obscures is the essential meaning. It is not just a question of the mode of expression but the semantic structure through which the message is communicated. It is at this deeper level that we must consider the present crisis in doctrinal and kerygmatic language.

II

In certain circles, the practice of theology as it has traditionally been conceived has been written off and we must examine the reasons for this. It is said that the present "crisis in theology" is

[1] Paul Ricoeur, *Critique de la Religion et Langage de la Foi* (stencilled lectures given at Lille, 1969).

really due to modern man's concern with scientific objectivity. In his concern with rationality, modern man has no time for the kind of metaphysical speculation, to which theology gave so much impetus, and which is alien to any notion of theological positivism. The people of whom we are talking are particularly concerned to put an end to the kind of mystical indifference which disregards objective reality. Jürgen Moltmann has described the process, inaugurated by the French Revolution whereby the earlier institutionary structures and their metaphysical foundations has crumbled.[2] What has disappeared is the consensus which offered a cultural and intellectual rationale by which all could live. Moreover, a chasm has undoubtedly appeared in what previous generations described as the "given" nature of Christian revelation. Any preconceived notion of truth has become completely suspect and is thought to be incapable of bearing much relation to reality. The growth of the human sciences have resulted in a questioning of the fundamental nature of theology itself, for it entails a deep study of the cultural basis of Christian preaching.

In turn, there seems to be a tendency to disqualify the transcendent aspects of dogma for it carries with it what Moltmann has called a supratemporality in which God's truth, either in relation to revelation or eschatology, is regarded as the epiphany of the eternal present and not the apocalyse of the promised future.[3] The notion of the self-revelation of God himself is quite alien to modern man with his awareness of the historically incomplete and evolutionary nature of the world. In so far as the teaching of the Church does not relate to this awareness, it is seriously questioned, if not actually refuted.

III

But this crisis of theology is in fact part and parcel of the religious crisis as a whole in the Western world. The more scientific and technical progress affect the economic and social situation the more there seems to be open to men the possibility of a total explanation of the natural and historical process. In spite of the

[2] Jürgen Moltmann, *Theology of Hope* (London, 1967), quoting Karl Barth.

[3] Jürgen Moltmann, *op. cit.*

obvious drawbacks of such a dependence upon rationality, this mood is very widespread. It is not just in intellectual circles that scientific thought has taken its hold—it has begun to take hold of the collective conscience as well. Indeed had not the word "scientific" come to be used in a pejorative sense (especially in theological circles), the process of secularization might have become complete. Naturally the study of reality in its social and natural aspects is bound to result in a reductionist attitude towards the credibility of a supernatural force and is equally bound to exclude the possibility of intervention by that force in the natural and historical process. Although the scientific method is a useful safeguard in the realms of intellectual knowledge, it does of course confound any attempt to talk of truth "from on high" for it will allow for nothing that cannot be verified by its own criteria. The present intellectual climate with its categories of what is possible, what is operative and what is verifiable simply ignores all the forces in our contemporary society which are irrational or utopian. Moreover, religion is completely excluded as a force to be taken into account in achieving a social consensus. Of course, it should be pointed out that anyone who takes this point of view would be forced to consider the role of religion negatively as a force in history and in the development of society.[4]

In a recent article, Emile Poulat pointed out that "those very concepts of God, the supernatural, heaven and hell, Jesus, the Son of God, miracles and the devil which have been taken for granted for so long in the West have in fact given very little impetus to the disruptive forces in society. Even today, they have been discounted as in any sense fundamental to the political order as it exists and to which they subscribe. The social consensus rests on other more general principles which have slowly and often painfully evolved and which have been influenced in no way by Christian revelation with its concept of salvation history. . . . So the fact remains that the supernatural is something which the individual may subscribe to but which is in no way determinant of the laws of society."[5]

---

[4] This is based on an idea provided by A. Gramsci.
[5] Emile Poulat, *Catholicisme urbain et pratique religieuse (Archives de Sociologie des Religions*, 29) (1970).

The doctrinal and kerygmatic crisis in the Church, then, is the result of a confrontation between two types of rationality. On the one hand, there is the theological and metaphysical type and on the other the scientific and technical. But it is also related to a social crisis which is affecting the Church as a whole. A breach has been opened in the fabric of the Christian interpretation of the world and a deep division has appeared between the religious consensus and the social consensus. It is these that have shaken the very foundation on which the preaching of the Christian gospel was based. The structure through which the Christian gospel has been communicated for centuries has been shattered and I suggest that the real reason for this has been the change in the Church's political position.

IV

The history of the Church in the last two hundred years has been characterized by a gradual decrease in its social influence and this on many fronts—political, judicial, economic and intellectual. In recent times, the Church has found that its social status was in some sense "extraterritorial". This process seems to be continuing unabated. If the Church has not been exactly absent, its influence upon the forming of political and social principles has been negligible. What we have witnessed is the corrosion of the Church's authority to talk to the fundamentally secular modern world. In those instances where this has not been the case, the Church has been the uncritical observer if not the accomplice of social and political orders which many would suspect and despise. We can only outline this process here. It must be enough to concentrate on those elements which are central to our thesis and which may offer some insight into how the Church may be led to offer a radical political critique of our modern world.

The Church *should* be doing this at every level. Its mission continually to reinterpret the primitive kerygma is particularly relevant to our thesis that preaching the gospel must be "situationally determined".[6] Even the dogmatic definitions of the

[6] This formula is taken from Karl Mannheim, *Idéologie et Utopie* (Paris, 1956).

Church, so long presented as the work of the Holy Spirit, are themselves conditioned by social and cultural circumstance in so far as it is these which have determined their formulation. Equally their expression must be conditioned by the pastoral situation and this in turn must qualify in some sense the once and for all nature of dogmatic definition as the Church has hitherto conceived it.

This "sociological" approach to theological discourse and dogmatic definition does raise fundamental questions about the Church as an institution and the world in which it exists. This has been little explored in the past though this is not true of the social teaching of the Church. In the past, sociologists such as Ernst Troeltsch have followed this line in order to point to the connivance between the Church and the society of which it is part.

Any consideration of the present doctrinal crisis must be part of an evaluation of the nature and purpose of the pastoral mission of the Church's teaching office. We must continually set the theory of the institutional Church against the praxis of the concrete pastoral situation in which it finds itself. Yves Congar in his notes on the Second Vatican Council suggested that we should aim at a pastorally orientated theology determined by the Church's pastoral needs. "If there is a crisis in the systematic reflection of the Church on her role in the world",[7] it is because of the corrosion of the Church's status in society. In turn, this can also be seen as the undermining of the traditional models that have been used to convey religious meaning and also of the sense in which theologians have talked of "God considered in Himself and in His work, which is by nature continually creative and saving".[8]

It is this which is the basic question underlying all dogmatic definition and the articulation of the orthodox faith, especially in so far as these determine the Church's directives and pastoral instructions. It is this that should now be subjected to the refining fire of sociological criticism.

It is precisely the claim that Christian teaching is independent of cultural and social conditioning that is so significant. Its claim

[7] A definition of pastoral theology provided by Pierre Adnes, *La Théologie Catholique* (Paris, 1967).
[8] Pierre Adnes, *op. cit.*

to universality demonstrates so forcibly its disregard of its true function in society. Maybe this is only true in varying degrees but nevertheless Christian discourse claims to propound a system which "possesses its own logic, its own intellectual discipline, its own language of images, myths and concepts and which is assured of a permanent role in whatever society it happens to be expounded."[9] Thus doctrinal language is firmly rooted in the religious sphere and is equally firmly linked to man's hope and nostalgia for a future life.

V

If, as we suggest, doctrinal and kerygmatic language should be seen as the product of a particular society, then these must be evaluated within the context of the social environment for which they are intended. It is the expression of religious truth designed to be normative at one particular time and is designed as the regulative statement of the Church of that time. Theological formulations of this nature are designed to express some kind of religious meaning in terms which make sense to the intellectual and social climate of the time. Thus it can no longer be a question of theological exposition based uniquely on the study of Scripture and the Early Fathers. This approach should be rejected by theologians today for, if doctrinal statements are made in tune with the intellectual climate of the time, then the essential content of such statements must be self-authenticating and the continual "shaking-up" of doctrinal statements becomes essential.

Of course, it is not a question of being completely pragmatic about theological ideals for this would hamper the emergence of new categories of thought. In fact, what we are proposing is a kind of hermeneutics arising from a complicity between doctrinal ideals and the exigencies of preaching the gospel in such a way as to allow for the continual reinterpretation of the Scriptures themselves. Thus, in interpreting Scripture, we should hope to achieve a direct confrontation between the ideals and demands of the Christian gospel and the practical and social exigencies of the Church at any given time.[10]

[9] Louis Althusser, *Pour Marx* (Paris, 1964), pp. 238–242.
[10] Antoine Casanova, *Vatican II et l'évolution de l'Eglise* (Paris, 1969).

It is in this continual dynamic tension between traditional theology and new religious categories that a healthy synthesis will be born. But the real problem for us is to know whether this tension can indeed function in a society where religion no longer forms part of the fabric of contemporary culture, and where a religious rationale of the future and purpose of man has disappeared from the minds of people as a whole. Does this really make sense in a world where there is no longer a consensus between the religious order and the social order?

VI

However inadequate the dynamic tension that we have been discussing may be, it certainly fulfils a regulating function in theological formulations. It takes many different forms. It can, for instance, be seen in the tension between popular religious belief, sometimes quite inadequately articulated, and the Church's own formulations which are often seen to come "couched in terms which are outdated in comparison with the reality they are attempting to express".[11] One has only to think for example of those grass-root movements which grow alongside the traditional structures of the parish, which are so often out of keeping with the demands of urban life. But underlying all this there seems to be an even more fundamental tension between the Church as a power structure and the Church as a social entity. In some cases it is precisely this reaction on the part of most believers, at least in small groups, against the power structure of the Church in its institutional form which can result in genuine reform from below. This has been the case for example with some underground movements in the Church. But in general there has been throughout the history of the Church a strong anti-institutional force in tension with the power structure itself. This power conflict within the Church has often come to the surface in theological debate and in this way the aspirations of the Church at the grass roots are articulated and the authority of the teaching office is challenged. After all, we only have to think of Vatican II where some of the theologians who had formerly been silenced by

[11] A definition provided by Mannheim, *op. cit.*, who insists that ideology is different from utopia, which could in theory become reality.

church authorities now appeared to the world at large as theological experts! If nothing else, this does show that the institutional Church can learn from the struggles among its rank and file members. This in no way compromises the status of the institution of the Church itself.

But what happens when the status and the role of the Church is threatened by the social order upon which it depends for its existence? Should it attempt to smother the ferment, to control the activities of theologians, to use the magisterium as a trump card and to walk a tight rope between concession and repression. For it is in this way that the Church has preserved its sense of superior religious vision, its claim to determine what is normative.[12] In this way it has been possible for the institutional Church to make doctrinal development and new ways of expressing the Christian gospel conform to its own theological models. It can thus preserve itself and maintain its role in the world.

I have tried to demonstrate that, in matters pertaining to man's various approaches to God, God's work in history and the mission of the Church to the world, the Church can be seen to operate through a kind of *a posteriori* rationalization. But I repeat that the question is does this hold good in a world where the Church is politically and socially on the fringe. Is not the present crisis in doctrinal and kerygmatic language symptomatic of the social disintegration of the Church?

VII

One thing is certain, any analysis by the theologian of the role of the Church in society now makes a degree of desacralization imperative, for only this will get to the roots of the crisis with which we are concerned. Whenever we scrutinize the theological opinions and doctrines of men at any particular time we detect

---

[12] When we use the term "connivance" here it should not be assumed that we are unaware that this process can indeed be a means of the Church maintaining its power. It concerns a discourse which is mysterious as well as mystifying. If, as Louis Althusser says in *Pour Marx, op. cit.*, "the function of ideology is never purely instrumental", those people who make ideology the inspiration for action may find that they are prisoners of the ideology which they thought they controlled. This is no less true in the context of which we are talking.

"under the idealized language of religion, the existence of deep human interest and of tensions between men as individuals and the society in which they live. The language of the theologians is the idealized and purified expression of these interests and these tensions."[13] We cannot just condemn this analysis of Christian language as reductionist. The Christian message is structurally tied to the culture which is the vehicle of its expression and the fact is that today it finds it hard to perform its role as ideology. But this is determined by the social position of the Church which is endorsing it. It is all too easy to see therefore how Christian language is nothing more nor less than the means of the Church justifying its existence on some ideological plane, while in fact it is conditioned by the existing political-economic order. Theology and the preaching of the gospel also in their own way reflect the conditioning of the body ecclesiastical by the body politic and the price the Church has paid for this since Constantine is that its social and political status is determined by the civil society in which it exists. Small wonder therefore that it has been the continual concern of orthodox theology to encourage a policy of submission and this has often been at the expense of the messianic and apocalyptic content of the Christian gospel. For this reason, I would argue that the religious emancipation of Christians constitutes a decisive step in their political emancipation. That is to say that the apparent harmony between Christian language and contemporary intellectual fashion is itself the reason for the crisis in doctrine and the preaching of the gospel.

It is not enough to point to the contradictions in the Church and especially to the polemics between traditional theology and the so-called new theologies in order to hasten the political and ideological emancipation of the Church. This is one of the illusions of those who attempt to reshape Christian language and thereby think that they are solving the problem of the Church's socially ambiguous position. In fact quite the reverse is true. Many of the so-called counter-theologies which attempt to transform traditional theology only seem to maintain the structure of the institutional Church as it is. This led Leo Dullart to write, "the theology of secularization only serves to reinforce the *raison*

[13] Lucien Sebag, *Marxisme et Structuralisme* (Paris, 1964).

d'être of our society, based as it is on the pursuit of financial profit, for it merely offers to Christians a theological justification for joining in the pursuit".[14] So often the new movements in Christian theology turn out to be no more than the adaptation of current ideological concerns to the needs of the social system of which it is a product—in our case advanced capitalism.

It is clear that the effectiveness of our theological language is today being corroded on two fronts. On the one hand it is threatened by the corrosion of the ideals of a bourgeois, liberal and individualistic society (a corrosion promoted by a revolution in social thought which is basically anti-religious) and on the other hand it is corroded by its endorsement of advanced capitalism which no longer needs theology to justify itself. Jean Guichard, taking up the themes in Moltmann's *Theology of Hope*, points to the emergence of various personalist and existentialist theologies at precisely the time when the structures of modern capitalism require "an interiorized religion which will put no spanner in the works of the basic social structures of our time . . . and freed from any association with a faith that they no longer need to endorse their existence and on the other hand a religion which offers to man relief from the increasing depersonalization of modern living".[15]

This double corrosion poses the essential problem in considering the crisis which this article has been describing. It is no longer a question of finding a theological alternative, of elaborating theological language in such a way as to make it acceptable to modern man dominated as he is by scientific and technical culture. It is rather a question of a point of departure for the theologian from which he should formulate the current religious ideology.

In fact at the moment the role of the theologian, cut off as he is from the great majority of Christian people, seems to be among those intellectuals whom Nizan described rather unkindly as the watch dogs of the ecclesiastical establishment. Many claim that our scholars seem quite incapable of making any genuine contribution to renewing the language of faith and would prefer the

[14] Leo Dullart, *Les Deux Visages de la Théologie de la Secularisation* (Paris, 1970), pp. 133 ff.
[15] Jean Guichard, *Eglise, Luttes de Classes et Stratégies Politiques* (Paris, 1972), p. 71.

centre of theological power to move down to the level of those communities where religious language is drawn from their own experience of the nature and purpose of their Christian existence. This necessitates a devolution of power in the Church which would in turn have its repercussions in the secular world as a whole. But it does not in itself guarantee the future role of Christian doctrine and the kerygma. For the future of theological language is the future of the Church and the Christian community as a whole and if it is true that the survival of any organization is intimately linked to its ability to maintain solidarity with the majority of its members in their struggle for liberation, then it is upon this very solidarity that the possibility of speaking of God depends today.

Translated by Robin Baird-Smith

Edward Schillebeeckx

The Crisis in the Language of Faith as a Hermeneutical Problem

I. The Historical Contingency of the Language of Faith

SINCE the Christian revelation is God's saving act as something experienced and expressed by believers who are, in this sense, "pious",[1] historically conditioned language plays an essential part in it. It is interpreted in the New Testament in terms such as redemption, the kingdom of God, the Son of Man, and so on, in other words, in the language of faith taken over from pre-Christian society and given a Christian meaning in the light of the historical event of Jesus, thus making that revelation a linguistic event. The Christian revelation, then, can only be approached by us as a reality expressed in an historically conditioned language of faith. This language of faith is not simply a mode of expression clothing an event which believers in the past were able to accept as a pure reality. On the contrary, the interpretative linguistic element is an essential aspect of revelation itself. There is no zone which is free from the changes that take place in language. There is a special historical contingency of the language of faith, just as there is a contingency of the historical event of Jesus. The language of the Bible therefore cannot be "translated" into contemporary language as though it were a child's game of changing a doll's clothes. The problem of Christian hermeneutics

[1] I have developed this idea more fully in the introduction to my article on "The Problem of the Infallibility of Office", *Concilium*, March 1973 (American Edn., vol. 83).

is far more complicated than that of language and translation with the language of the Bible as the ultimate criterion.

As a man, Jesus of Nazareth was placed in a contingent event of time—that of the history of the Jewish people who interpreted themselves as the people of God, serving and bearing witness to God in the world. In this—interpreted—history, Jesus had his own special task to carry out, but was confronted by many already existing and widely differing interpretations of the concepts "people" and "kingdom" of God. Among the most important were, for example, the apocalyptical, the eschatological, the ethical and the mystical interpretations, as well as the political interpretation of the Zealots. Jesus defined his own, very personal standpoint within this variety of interpretations, although his death made his message and choice of attitude historically ambiguous. Quite apart from the Church's kerygma or creed, this may be seen as a concise expression of the results achieved by careful historical research into the sources.

We must therefore be careful not to lose sight of this historical contingency of Jesus' appearance when we are speaking in the language of faith about Jesus as the Messiah, the Son of Man, the Lord, and so on. We should also not make the biblical expression of Jesus' words and actions in those concrete circumstances unhistorical and absolute by dissociating it from the historically conditioned linguistic categories of the period in which the event of Jesus was expressed. The linguistic event should not, in other words, be raised to the level of "timeless" categories. The multiplicity of christological dogmas and the different definitions of the kingdom of God, redemption, and so on, in the New Testament itself should be sufficient warning against this practice.

These original creeds are historically ambiguous in their language and, because they are so diverse, they are also conditioned by the historical ambiguity of the concrete phenomenon of Jesus and the fact that it is not diaphanous to human reason. The gospel of Mark clearly aims to safeguard this non-diaphanous quality of the historical event of Jesus by making use of the so-called "messianic mystery". The same is done in the canonical version of the Fourth Gospel, in sharp contrast to the source used, the so-called "miracle narratives", which present us with an al-

most compellingly visible form of Jesus' divinity. The historical
ambiguity of the phenomenon of Jesus, which is open to so many
interpretations, appears to anyone reading the New Testament
writings against the background of the "non-canonical" oral and
written pre-history of the New Testament, which was often ex-
tended into later "apocryphal" gospels, to be a consensus of all
the canonical writings which interpret Jesus, perhaps in many
different ways, as the one Jesus in the light of the kerygma of
his death and resurrection.

The problem of the language of faith, then, presents us with a
conflict between the historical ambiguity of Jesus' life, work and
death on the one hand and, on the other, the religious and social
expectations, aspirations and ideologies from which what was
expressed in Jesus himself was made historically concrete in the
New Testament and the history of the Church.[2] Only in the
second place is it a question of a translation into our contemporary culture of the authentic reality of Jesus distilled from this
conflict. The relationship with the constantly changing history
with its distinctive culture is therefore inherent in the Christian
creed and in the whole language of Christian faith.

The Christian who takes the confession of faith, "Jesus Christ,
the Lord of history", seriously will at once understand that our
relationship with our own contemporary historical situation will
naturally play a part in what we have to say in the language of
faith about Jesus Christ and his Church. To refuse to acknowledge this fact and to make the language of faith of a given
period, even that of the New Testament, absolute would be to
deny that Jesus is the Lord of all history, including our own.
Speaking in the language of faith, then, is essentially an historical
and hermeneutical undertaking. Anyone who denies the historicity of the Christian faith and its language and therefore
denies the necessity of this hermeneutical undertaking will inevitably—but mistakenly—believe that a crisis in the language of
faith is a crisis of faith as such and, by polarization, force a state
of crisis in the Church. On the other hand, the Christian who is
aware of the different languages of faith and of the many re-
interpretations of Jesus even in the New Testament—all of them,

[2] See E. Schillebeeckx, "De toegang tot Jezus van Nazaret", *Tijdschrift
voor Theologie*, 12 (1972), pp. 28–60, especially pp. 56 ff.

however, confessing faith, perhaps from a different vantage point, in the one Jesus of Nazareth—will realize that we are certainly experiencing a crisis in the language of faith today, but will not regard this process of identification as such as the collapse of the Christian faith itself. (The canonization of very differing early Christian writings in the language of faith did not, for instance, imply a crisis of faith in the past.) As a Christian, he will regard this as an attempt on the part of his fellow believers to express in a critical relationship with the present what was revealed in Jesus, in other words, to express that revelation in faithfulness to Jesus and yet in a different language of faith within the framework of a changed experience of man and the world which has become the flesh and blood of contemporary man's life.

In faithfulness, but in twentieth-century language, Christians are trying today to answer the question: "But who do you say that I am?" (Mark 8. 29; Matt. 16. 15; Luke 9. 20) and this involves an element of risk. It is also, however, evidence of considerable vitality.

II. The Language of Faith—not a Ghetto Language

1. Like every language, the language of faith is not a "metaphysical factor". On the contrary, it is the expression of both sense and nonsense in our concrete, human social history. It is not only the possibility of expression, however, but also the possibility of alienation and "ideology", the place where salvation is found and where it is also absent. Like all use of language, speaking in the language of faith may at any time be suspected of "ideology", in other words, it may be speaking in a fragmented relationship with reality, an abusive use of language in the abuse of power.

The language of faith is made of precisely the same stuff as our ordinary human language is made of, language as a "lifeform" (Wittgenstein) and as a social reality. There is no special ghetto language of faith. If it exists as a ghetto language, then it is in this case an anachronistic relic of what was once the everyday, universally intelligible language of human society which had become separated and had ceased to develop along

with the rest of human language and had thus become the ghetto
language of an enclosed "in" group, intelligible only to this group
and to experts. But, since the members of this group or community cannot, in Western society at least, live in a totally isolated
ghetto, but are bound to participate in the life of society as a
whole, their own ghetto language is bound eventually to become
a problem to those who use it, in this case, the believers,[3] who
are experiencing an acute crisis in the "language of faith", on
the basis of social isolation and marginality. Even though it
would be wrong to regard this as a religious dismantling of the
"in" group, to use this particular language of faith in isolation
deprives it of its evangelical force and makes it a threat to real
religiosity.

Language, including that of faith, becomes meaningless, in the
sense in which linguistic analysts use the term, if it does not
contain a recognizable reference to man's experience in the
world.[4] There can, for example, be no real and meaningful possibility of people listening to the message of Christ's redemption
and of their being open to give their consent to it if that message
cannot be experienced and seen, in however fragmentary a way,
in our existence here on earth. Christian salvation is not, of
course, the same as our concept of pure humanity, but it is mani-
fested as a promise in the historical process of man's freedom,
just as Jesus, in going around doing good, gave concrete form to
his message of ultimate salvation. The message of redemption is
always threatened with the danger of becoming an "ideology"
if it cannot be experienced by man as concrete human freedom.

This is why it is always necessary to verify our speaking in the
language of faith against a careful analysis of individual and
social alienation and against the hermeneutics of human experience. If it is to be a language that we can understand, what is
said about Jesus the Christ in the history of the Church must be
recognizably related to our experience in society, in which it is
impossible to escape in practice the question of sense and nonsense. If this link with human experience is broken, the language

[3] See, for example, L. Gilkey, Naming the Whirlwind (Indianapolis,
1969).
[4] See E. Schillebeeckx, Glaubensinterpretation. Beiträge zu einer hermen-
eutischen und kritischen Theologie (Mainz, 1971), pp. 13–17.

of faith becomes unintelligible in its positive aspect of salvation and its negative aspect, the absence of salvation, and many people become indifferent to the decision for or against the Christian message.

Let me give two examples of this unintelligibility due, in the first case, to the absence of any connection between the language of faith and human experience and, in the second, to an uncritical adaptation to already existing data of human experience. In the first example, biblical and traditional speaking about the kingdom of God becomes unintelligible if the point of what that kingdom means to us is not translated or interpreted,[5] for the simple reason that the early "theocratic" view is no longer meaningful or acceptable to us in our present experience. The necessary critical message of this kingdom of God is denied to modern man if it is not translated into his language. As a second example, I would take the term "God is Father", which has become problematical for quite a different reason. The hermeneutics of experience has, through a psychological process of purification, shown the father-relationship to be an anthropological structure.[6] This inevitably means that there will be a crisis in our experience of faith of the term "God is Father", because we live in a "fatherless" society. The solution to *this* problem of crisis in the language of faith cannot, however, be found in doing away with the religious father-concept. On the contrary, the solution is to criticize society and to change its structures, in order to give the language of faith, in this case the term "God is Father", a function in the criticism of society.

All religious movements, including the Church as the "movement around Jesus", are inextricably part of human society. The real question is whether sufficient critical and creative tension is being maintained between our speaking in the language of faith and the social environment in which we do it. The language of faith is not identical with speaking in the world, but its matrix is always a "secular" speaking within a disclosure experience of faith and together with an evocative and critical surplus.

[5] See, for example, O. H. Streck, "Prophetische Kritik der Gesellschaft", *Christentum und Gesellschaft* (Göttingen, 1969), pp. 46–62.
[6] See especially J.-M. Pohier, *Vers le Père* (Paris, 1972).

2. This clearly implies a rejection of all linguistic dualism, which is, of course, to be found in many spheres of human activity. This dualism is, however, especially prominent in connection with the Church and above all when a contrast is made between speaking sociologically about the Church and speaking transcendentally about the mystery of the Church. As believers, we must clearly also speak in the language of faith about the Church even when we are speaking about very ordinary aspects of the Church as a community subject to sociological laws, because it is, in its completely human character, also the community of God. On the other hand, however, it is not only a sterile abstraction, but also very often a dangerous ideology to condemn sociological speaking about the Church as alien and to speak only in the language of faith without discussing the secular structures of the Church at all. This is clearly a "docetic" way of speaking about the Church and thus subject to criticism in the light of the empirical and analysable aspects of the Church. There is, of course, a difference between speaking in the language of faith and speaking sociologically about the Church, but both ways of speaking refer to the same reality, with the result that there is no safe zone left over for a dualistic and therefore "supernaturalistic" language of faith. Relating to the same reality, both language games are complementary to each other.

The right of the so-called "two-language approach"—the language of faith and secular speaking, that is, sociological, scientific or historical language—is indisputable, but it is most important not to forget that it is the same reality that is approached and interpreted, although from different points of view and with different questions. To forget this would be disastrous for both approaches because of the danger that the language of faith may become an ideology, possibly in order to justify uncritically accepted social processes in which the Church has become involved.

The classic solution to the problem of "faith and science" was found in a rather facile distinction, namely, that the facts were the concern of science and that faith was concerned with the meaning of the facts. This seemed to do justice to both aspects— a special sphere for the sciences, which were thus not hindered by faith, and a special sphere for faith, which thus remained im-

mune to science. The consequence of this distinction, however, was
that the sphere of scientific facts became wider and wider, first
in the cosmos, then in the biological world, and finally in man
himself and his psyche. On the other hand, however, theologians
felt that the real ground of facts were being swept from under
their feet. Since then, the ideological aspect of this distinction
between the sphere of facts and the sphere of meaning has been
exposed by sociologists, psychiatrists and others whose sciences
were both analytical and hermeneutic. Scientists, then, were
active in the sphere of meaning, while theologians had the feeling that their study was vanishing into thin air. In the mean-
time, the idea had for a long time prevailed that God was alien
to the sphere of facts and reason. The basic concept of creation
withered away and theology became pure eschatology—a variety
of theologies of hope flourished without any foundation of creation. Even theological hermeneutics became more and more alienated from the facts.

The crisis in the language of faith, then, is partly the result
of the "two-language approach", in so far as this theory fails to
take into account the fact that it is the same reality that is approached and interpreted, although it is viewed from different
standpoints. The sphere of facts must have enough pointers for
what is said in the "other sphere" in the language of faith to be
meaningful and intelligible despite its inexpressible surplus. It is,
above all, this surplus, which cannot be approached by reason,
that has to be expressed in the language of faith in the form of
parables and stories—in other words, the narrative element has to
be used for this surplus in the language of faith. These parables
and stories prevent us from identifying what has already been
achieved in our history and what still remains to be achieved
with the consummation at the end which is God's gift and
his affirmation of all that is good, holy and beautiful in history.
At the same time, they provide us with a set of models by means
of which the Christian community can see the character of God's
coming which preserves us both in conversion and in responsible
activity in our history. This promise is more than a mere criticism or negation of what is available. It orientates activity and
stimulates resolute but provisional activity that is averse to all
forms of totalitarianism and of premature "unification" in theory

or in praxis. All this is intimately connected with the authenticity of the language of faith.

I cannot go into the so-called conflict of the models of interpretation here, because this would take me too far from my intention of simply pointing out a dualism which is accepted by many Christians and which in fact perpetuates the crisis in the language of faith, especially in the various offshoots of Protestant "dialectical theology" and in the Catholic theology that is derived from it. One of the results of this dualism is the emergence of forms of theology which attempt to resolve the conflict by doing away with one of the two poles of the language of faith and using exclusively a secular way of speaking about faith. This, however, brings about a real crisis of *faith*. We may therefore conclude that there can be no living faith without a language of faith.

III. Not simply Language but also Praxis

It is common to speak of a disturbance in communication, in connection with the crisis in the language of faith, between the New Testament (the past) and ourselves in the present. This leads to an identification of the hermeneutical problem with this disturbance in communication, which is attributed to the distance either in time or in society.

It is, however, ambiguous to speak of "distance" in this context, because the New Testament is among us, for example, in the Church's proclamation here and now. The language of faith is therefore problematical in a very concrete form—the Church's claim that the Christian truth that is inherited from the past is still valid today. As long as we see the past, however, as a dead sediment, we shall remain at an abstract theoretical level at which we can only analyse formally the structure of our understanding of our historical experience. We also tend to assume *a priori* that there is no disturbance, but that there ought to be communication with the past. We think within a sphere of meaning which allows the present and the past to be seen as a continuous whole within a changing, widening horizon. As for the validity of this scheme of present-past, it is clear that the scheme itself implies an interpretation and a negative evaluation, in other words, the break between the past and the present is interpreted as a disturbance in communication, but no answer has been given to why this should be so. It has been suggested that, for the sake of the present and a better future, the past should be left as past, because—following the reasoning of the Enlightenment—the present is an emancipation from the past. But this, too, is an assumption and as such implies an interpretation. We are bound to conclude that it is not possible to uphold the abstract scheme of present-past, because, both in a negative and in a positive interpretation, the present and the past are mediated.

The consequence of this is that the universal question of communication—with which our special question, the language of faith, is intimately concerned—is always asked within a certain context of interpretation. Broadly speaking, there are three possible approaches. The first is that followed by J. Habermas, who views the past from the vantage point of a critical emancipation from a previous history that is authoritarian and, in that sense, violent. The second way of looking at the past, that of H.-G. Gadamer, is from the point of view of a history which is, in some way, normative for us. The third way is to approach the past in the light of a critical and selective remembrance of human traditions containing not only many irrelevant and even meaningless events, but also what N. Luhmann has called "sediments of meaning", many of which are extremely important for our decisions in the present about the future. This tendency of a critical *memoria praeteriti* is followed by several of the protagonists of the so-called "critical theories" including J. Habermas and also by such thinkers as H. Marcuse, Kolakowski, P. Ricoeur, J. B. Metz and W. Oelmüller. We may therefore conclude that any consideration of the crisis in the language of faith, of communication and of disturbance in communication includes an interpretation, with the result that the hermeneutical problem cannot be separated from the so-called criticism of ideology. Understanding in and through language, including that of faith, is therefore bound to be not only a question of hermeneutics, but also a criticism of ideology.

Let me illustrate this with one example, that of "redemption". An essential aspect of the evangelical concept of redemption is the call to conversion or *metanoia*. But does this call not become an ideology if it is limited merely to an inner conversion and if the conditions under which this can be realized are absent and especially if the subject to be changed, man not simply as a logical being, but also as a social being who acts, is not realistically defined? Within the context of such questions, speaking in the language of faith about redemption is seen to be closely related to man's commitment to a truly human emancipation from many kinds of personal and social alienation. This emancipation motivated by genuine care for our fellow men and carried out, for example, by those who are active in the spheres of mental and spiritual welfare and social or political work can be seen as a sign and an *arrha* of salvation, although they are not identical.

This, of course, poses all kinds of questions, including, for example, the political implications of the message of salvation and the dialectical tension between inner conversion and social or political reform. Both a purely private language of faith and one which never expresses the mystical element cease to be intelligible and forfeit their critical function with regard to the tendencies to make society more and more private on the one hand and increasingly scientific and technocratic on the other. This new historical situation undoubtedly requires us to test once again our speaking in the language of faith about redemption or freedom.[7]

Soteriological language—speaking about redemption—thus includes both the language of freedom and the language of liturgical celebration and consequently points to praxis and action—or is at least a "performative" language, calling for action—and to our liturgical thanking of God for his redemption which through men of goodwill on earth anticipates the signs of this salvation.[8] Religiosity forms an essential part of the language of faith, which is therefore always doxological, that is, praising God on the one hand, and "performative" with regard to social and political commitment on the other. If these two aspects are

---

[7] Successful attempts to speak, in faithfulness to the gospel, in a new language of faith about the "kingdom of God" and "redemption" have been made by R. Pesch, *Von der "Praxis des Himmels"* (Graz, 1971) and H. Kessler, *Erlösung als Befreiung* (Düsseldorf, 1972).

[8] See my paper in the report on the congress held at Nijmegen University, 20–23 March 1972.

separated, the language of faith will become an ideology and the critical commitment of the Christian community will become a theological duplication of what is already being done successfully by those who do not belong to the Church.

IV. THE LANGUAGE OF FAITH AND CRITICAL REMEMBRANCE OF THE PAST

One of the many aspects of the crisis in the language of faith is a tendency, since Adolf Harnack, among Protestants to regard the history of Christianity since its origin as a decline and a corresponding tendency among Roman Catholics to justify that history as a necessary organic development.[9] If Christianity really had its origin in Jesus of Nazareth and the response of his disciples to his appearance, then this origin must inevitably be a lasting criterion for the language of faith. It has to be admitted, however, that any pre-critical idealism based on this origin is also pernicious, since the New Testament language of faith, the structures of the primitive Christian community were also mediated by the contingent circumstances of the time—the normative revelation is not provided in its pure form by this origin.

Since our relationship with the past is in itself an option for the future and never purely theoretical, the alternative definition suggested by some of those who have considered this question, namely that, in our attempt to find a new language of faith, there is no theoretical mediation between the past and the present, but a mediation in praxis between the present and the future, strikes me as false. Our relationship with the future is, after all, mediated by our relationship with the past, just as our definite remembrance of the past is mediated by a definite plan for the future. This is why we refer, correctly, to critical and definite memories of the past. An option for a concrete memory of the history of man's suffering is therefore subject to the choice of a plan for the future in which a better history is regarded as possible and necessary for those who suffer and die or are poor and without rights. The fact that our relationship with the past is

[9] J. Ratzinger, *Das Problem der Dogmengeschichte in der Sicht der katholischen Theologie* (Cologne and Opladen, 1966), pp. 8–15.

never purely theoretical has certain consequences for our speaking in the language of faith.

Our attempt to find a new language of faith that is humanly relevant and intelligible cannot be justified by a direct appeal to the New Testament, the "origin". (This proved to be the case in the past as well, in connection with the Church's traditional language of faith.) Biblical language has the task of orientating other languages of faith, both traditional and new, and it has a critical function with regard to them, but it cannot justify them. A language of faith can only be based indirectly and historically on the language of the Bible and this is because it can be shown that a relationship with social, political, religious and popular philosophical ideas of the period played an important part in the biblical language of faith. An authentic language of faith can therefore only be justified indirectly by reference to the language of the Bible.

What was regarded as possible and legitimate by the biblical authors for the expression of the New Testament faith in Jesus Christ in different social situations cannot be denied to Christians at a later period in the history of the Church. This is, indirectly, where the biblical basis of a new language of faith is to be found, both in praxis—for example, a more democratic exercise of authority by the Church—and in theory—for example, redemption as emancipation from all forms of human alienation. Neither the traditional nor the modern language of faith can therefore be made absolute. The question concerning a new language of faith which will express what we, under pressure of the reality of Jesus, mean by that reality now in our search for freedom in a world worthy of man today arises again and again in different social and political situations.

The difficulty of this inevitable question can be found in a choice. Should we project only our contemporary categories, still used in the criticism of society, on to this Jesus, thereby creating an unnecessary theological duplication of an already perfectly meaningful praxis? On the other hand, should we subject ourselves at the same time to criticism by the reality of Jesus in our use, in the criticism of society, of these contemporary categories in order to express Jesus in them? This would apply both in so far as the reality of Jesus is the focal point of a living community of faith which is directed towards God and man and which confesses him in prayer and in praxis as the Lord of history and in so far as this reality is increasingly shown by an historical approach to be seen as "Jesus of Nazareth". The difficulty of this hermeneutical undertaking is to be found in the circle in which it takes place. It is to be found in the first place in our need to express this reality of Jesus in categories which are already given to us, but at the same time in the fact that we can only come to know what this reality means to us now by using these categories. In the second place, the hermeneutical difficulty also exists whether or not our option for the future, within which we put questions to the Bible, is itself subject to the criticism of the evangelical promise. This is a fundamental hermeneutical conflict and one which is critical of ideology. Our modern speaking in the language of faith is bound to take place within this conflict.

In conclusion, I would like to point to the inevitably experimental character of any period of crisis in the language of faith, as at present, when there can be no purely scientific guarantee of automatic success. How should Christians react to this hazardous situation? We should, I think, above all have trust in the faith of our Christian communities and in the presence of the Holy Spirit in them. Mistakes will inevitably occur. It is clear that, in the New Testament, pre-canonical oral and written traditions were corrected by the canon of Scripture, which had to rely on those traditions in order to achieve a new language of faith in a changed situation and that the New Testament itself contains a very large number of different corrections. This knowledge should help to dispel all anxiety. In addition to this vigilant trust in the guidance of the Spirit, we should also remain open to evangelical admonition, especially in cases when the Christian community is experiencing difficulty in recognizing a particular form of theological speaking as the language of faith. There is also a constant need for evangelical encouragement among those whose hazardous task it is to translate the Christian message critically yet faithfully for the modern world. Finally, in exceptional cases, however risky it may be, we must be prepared to pronounce a *non possumus* if the being or non-being of Christianity is at stake.

If Christians react in this way to the present crisis in the language of faith resulting from great social change, they should not experience any real crisis of faith itself. On the contrary, their faith in Jesus of Nazareth as expressed in the language of faith should be purified and strengthened with the critical help of theology. In a world which they often experience, rightly, as with disillusionment and suffering, they are bound to ask: "Lord, to whom shall we go?" (John 6. 68).

Translated by David Smith

Harald Weinrich

Narrative Theology

I

IN those days Jesus of Nazareth gathered tax collectors and sinners around him and told them a story. "Once upon a time," he began, "there lived a man who had a hundred sheep. One day one of the sheep was lost. The man left the flock on its own and went off to look for the lost sheep. After a long time and much trouble he found it, happily put it on his shoulders and brought it back to the flock."

Now among the audience was a young woman who was carrying a purse with money in it. While Jesus was telling his story a coin fell out of her purse and rolled away. She immediately jumped up and ran after the coin until she caught it. The rest of the audience looked very severe and said to Jesus, "Sir, tell this woman not to distract us while we're listening."

Jesus smiled and told them another story. "Many years ago there lived a woman who had ten drachmas. One day she lost one drachma. She searched through the whole house and shone a light into every corner until at last she found the coin she had lost. Full of joy, she called all her friends and neighbours together and told them the good news of how she had found the drachma."

II

What have I just been doing? I have been telling a story. I'm afraid, though, that my story may have caused a double scandal. First, I have produced an apocryphal gospel. As everyone knows,

46

the message of Jesus has been announced once and for all, and not
a jot of it may now be changed. Second, I have told a story in an
academic journal. You don't tell stories in academic journals, you
argue. Take for example *Concilium* for September 1970, which
was devoted to the subject "Church History at a Turning Point".
Even the titles of the contributions show that arguments, not
stories, are to be expected: "Church History and the Reorienta-
tion of the Scientific Study of History", "Towards a Displacement
of Historicism and Positivism", "Church History in the Context
of the Human Sciences", and so on. So my hi-story will, I'm afraid,
be a rare exception in this journal. And even I, with my story
hardly over, am already beginning to argue. . . .

To begin with, an apologetic argument. Why shouldn't I tell
stories in an academic journal if Jesus of Nazareth spent a good
part of his public life telling stories? I will be even more precise.
He told and retold stories. He did not make up the story of the
lost sheep himself, but found it in another storyteller, the prophet
Ezekiel (Ezek. 34. 5–6), and we cannot even say for certain
whether Ezekiel was the first to tell it. Jesus passes on the story
by retelling it. If we now compare the two stories, we find that
they do not agree word for word. Retelling therefore doesn't
mean literal repetition; its meaning includes altering the text;
this is allowed within limits and is even a normal part of the
genre. Immediately after, in the biblical text (Lk. 15), we find the
story of the lost coin. The evangelist implies that this story is also
connected in tradition with the story of the lost sheep. The story
of the lost coin can also be seen as a retelling. It transposes the
story of the lost sheep from its setting in a pre-monetary economic
system (where sheep were the standard units of exchange) into a
literary form appropriate to a monetary economy.[1] In the language
of linguistics, this is a case of the common phenomenon of metaphor modernization producing a variant of a story within a
relatively fixed structure of tradition.

I have now devoted a moment to linguistic arguments, and if
I can also succeed in defending this literary thesis against all

[1] Bernhard Laum, *Heiliges Geld* (Tübingen, 1924). Cf. H. Weinreich,
"Münze und Wort. Untersuchungen an einem Bildfeld", in H. Lausberg
and H. Weinreich (ed.), *Romanica. Festschrift für G. Rohlfs* (Halle, 1958),
pp. 508–21.

48   HARALD WEINRICH

attempts at falsification, the rules of the academic game will be satisfied: *habemus veritatem*. Nevertheless I am still troubled by the question as to whether the story I told at the beginning does not contain the same truth, even though parts of this story were obviously my own invention. The story Jesus of Nazareth tells in Luke is, in both its pre-monetary and its monetary variants, a made-up story, a parable, and yet it never occurs to anyone that this is a reason for thinking it unimportant. The meaning of the story does not suffer from the story's indifference to historical fact. Similarly, from my reading of the Bible, I know of no case in which the disciples or other listeners asked the storyteller Jesus at the end of a story whether what he had said ever really happened. There is no trace of an historical interest in the truth of the story, in the sense of Ranke's "as it really was", either in the disciples' questions or in the Master's answers.[2]

For this reason, I cannot get away from the suspicion that the question about history in theology may be a false one. The biblical tradition seems to imply much more a question about stories. Whole sections of the texts canonized as the Bible, like many of the other oral and written texts of Christianity, are stories. The Bible does of course include in both Old and New Testaments texts of a different character, laws, moral precepts, rules of hygiene, letters of exhortation and expressions of praise and thanksgiving, but it is certainly no exaggeration to say that the most important texts, the ones most relevant to religion, are stories. Jesus of Nazareth is presented to us primarily as a person about whom stories are told, and frequently also as a person about whose storytelling stories are told, and the disciples appear as listeners to stories, who then spread and retell, orally or in writing, the stories they have heard. This is how the stories have come down to us, and when we retell the biblical stories to our children —if we are wise, we don't repeat them word for word—we too become part of an unbroken tradition of storytelling. Christianity is a community of storytellers. No doubt that is not an exhaustive definition; it is equally true to say that it is a community at table together. But after all the two are not so very different: in both

[2] Ranke, *Sämtliche Werke* (Leipzig, 2nd ed., 1874), vol. 33, pp. vi–vii.

cases everyone sits round, with the master of ceremonies in the middle, as in Leonardo's *Last Supper*.

III

We should try to imagine the circle of the apostolic storytelling community in as much detail as possible. The apostles and disciples, whom we must imagine as present in every case, form the inner circle of listeners. But the circle is not cut off from other listeners. Jesus told his stories in public, as we can still see storytellers doing in some societies today. As a rule, the stories were not interpreted but they were continued after the story circle broke up by being spread and retold by their hearers. The stories did not try to produce a clear yes or no as to truth, but more or less relevance. The most relevant stories are directed at faith: they want the hearer himself to imitate the actions of the story. In this process of reception and imitation, an explicit interpretation is not needed, and so even the poor in spirit, to the extent that they are of good will, can receive some benefit from the stories. If Jesus afterwards explains the deeper meaning of the story to his disciples ("I am that good shepherd"), as we often find him doing in the biblical reports, that is an *arcanum*, an exceptional privilege for the first, chosen retellers. By this means they receive in their youth instruction which normally only turns into the wisdom of age at the end of a long life and after listening to very many stories. Time presses when there is a world to be changed, and in this way these young people can become old before their time, elders, πρεσβύτεροι, priests.

In imitation of Christ, the storyteller from Nazareth about whom many stories were told, we can imagine a Christianity which transmits itself from generation to generation in an endless chain of retellings of stories: "faith comes by hearing". Any resulting change in the characters and situation of the story would be quite within the limits of narrative tolerance. It would therefore be no infringement of the laws of narrative if a story which in the beginning (but is there ever really a beginning in the storytelling tradition?) was about the killing of the children in Bethlehem was retold with a story of the persecution of the Jews in Nazi Germany or about the Vietnam war. Some people may

say that this is something different. It is true that these are
different stories, but these are just the sort of variations with
which a story circle can go from one story to another. One story is
not necessarily followed by an exactly similar story, or by a directly
contrary one, but, as in Boccaccio's *Decameron*, by a different
story in some way connected. The point of the story cannot be
extracted by an examination in terms of "true" and "false", but
becomes part of the wisdom of the ages as a succession of stories
gradually builds up our experience of life and salvation.

IV

Christianity, however, did not remain a storytelling community. In its meeting with the Hellenistic world it lost its poetic
innocence. In Greek culture, storytelling (myth) had long been
subordinate to argument (logos). We can see the subjection of the
mythmakers' stories to the arguments of the philosopher very
clearly in Plato's writings, even though Plato himself attempted
to give a new and philosophical brilliance to myth. On the whole,
however, Plato's attempt failed, and ever since philosophers have,
with increasing severity, refused to tell stories. It is true that
Augustine told the story of his life as confessions, Descartes told
of his philosophical method and Pascal called for the God of
Abraham, Isaac and Jacob (the God of the stories), Rousseau told
of the contradictions in human nature and Nietzsche tells the
story of the wisdom of Zarathustra. But on the other side are the
chariots of the other philosophers, who see their task as argument
and discussion, distinction and theory, and who cannot be per-
suaded at any price in the scientific world to let a story be a tale.
Telling stories, even listening to stories, counts in our society as
an unscientific occupation.[3]

V

This places theology and some other disciplines which I will
not list individually in a very weak position. Theology, of course,

[3] For further discussion of this, see my *Literatur für Leser* (Stuttgart,
1972), esp. the chapters "Erzählstrukturen des Mythos" and "Erzählte
Philosophie oder Geschichte des Geistes".

is faced with a more or less canonical body of texts, of which a large and important part is made up of stories. No wonder that scientific theologians could imagine no more urgent task than the transformation of the traditional stories as quickly and completely as possible into non-stories. For a time it even looked as though the opposite would happen, and that the argument itself would be turned into a story: "In the beginning was the word, and the word was with God. . . ." All the signals for a story are present in this text, just as in a proper—true or fictional—story. But in this aspect the Johannine prologue has remained barren. The logos was not turned into a story, but instead the biblical stories were turned into logos, an argument.

There is no need to describe this process in detail; one example of its work is the existence of theological journals such as *Concilium*, which also shows signs of the general and age-old tendency to drive narrative out of the Christian tradition through "demythologization". All forms of narrative? Here there is a slight difference between the two large Christian religious communities. Protestant theology as a rule has moved further away from stories than Catholic theology. But there is one strange thing. Even in the most logical demythologizing there remains one striking exception, the story of the Easter event. "He has risen". What does that mean, an event? Anyone who is used to listening to stories immediately hears the story signal: *Accidit ut . . .*, "It came to pass that . . ."—happening, hi-story, story. The Easter event formula in this way becomes simply an event about which a story is told, and one which sums up all the other events about which stories have been or could be told. But this central event can also produce a situation in which those who have accepted the story of the Easter event as hearers and in this quality acknowledge themselves as members of the Christian storytelling community in the Easter greeting "Christ is risen," are thereby dispensed from accepting or retelling any other stories. The Christian now only needs to retell the story of the Easter event, and no other, an important dispensation in a post-narrative age.

Let us now say something in more detail about which literary forms can count as stories in the Christian tradition. In the first place there are those stories—true or fictional—which a modern

sensitivity to literary forms recognizes as stories by particular
syntactic signals, especially narrative tenses and certain macro-
syntactic adverbs. One such story is that of the prodigal son ("A
man had two sons. The elder of them said to his father. . ."). We
may also count as a story a style of speaking in which, for
example, Luke reports the account of the lost sheep and the lost
coin ("Which of you who has a hundred sheep, if he lost one of
them, would not leave the other ninety-nine in the wilderness?").
This form could be called the hypothetical narrative: here possible
situations are described. Finally, the idea of storytelling, which
has already been separated from truth, should also be separated
from the past. The question Danto asks at the beginning of his
poem (and answers negatively), whether it is possible to tell the
story of an event that has not yet happened, must be answered by
theologians with a firm yes.[4] The prophecies in the biblical
corpus can be regarded as rough sketches in story form of actions
which have not yet taken place, as a pre-telling. The fulfilment
(or filling out) of the prophecy enriches the outline story with
elements of action which are then themselves re-told together
with the pre-told prophecy. It is well known that typological
structures of this sort, through which different stories are connected with one another, determined the early Christian attitude
to history, until modern profane history drove them out of the
Christian consciousness.[5]

VI

I have conducted my discussions so far—and this must be my
third occasion of scandal—as if I had never heard of the scientific
study of history. In what follows I will take the existence of this
discipline explicitly into account, and this will shift the ground
of our story problem slightly. Slightly, no more, because even the
scientific study of history contains an irreducible element of
stories. "History tells stories," says Danto. It is a *vera narratio*

[4] Arthur C. Danto, *Analytical Philosophy of History* (Cambridge, 2nd
ed., 1968).
[5] Cf. Erich Auerbach, "Figura", in *Gesammelte Aufsätze zur romanischen Philologie* (Berne, 1967), pp. 55–92.

(Bodin).[6] The science of history, however—and this is its tragedy —wants to tell only true stories and naturally stories with more than individual relevance. It has therefore concentrated a great deal of its theoretical energy on the question of how the truth of a story is to be found and protected against all falsification in the process of transmission.

Theology has been unable to escape from the influence of the scientific study of history, which increased steadily up to the nineteenth century. Theology has also begun to inquire with increasing urgency into the truth-content of its stories. It is open to discussion whether one should regard this process as beginning with doubts about the resurrection, which were answered not merely with a simple retelling, but with an "historical" assertion: "he really rose". Alternatively, the beginning of the alliance between theology and scientific history can be placed at the point where Christian theologians allowed historical textual criticism to be applied to biblical stories. However that may be, theology today is dominated by the unanimous and almost unquestioned view that the biblical stories, if they must be mentioned at all, should be allowed to stand as stories at the most when they can be proved by the recognized scientific methods of history to be true stories. This condition is, however, not easy to meet, especially where transcendence is concerned, and theology in its rearguard actions likes to take refuge in peripheral stories which are better able to satisfy the methodological principles of the science of history.[7] Theology engages—and here I quote from a theological essay— in form criticism, redaction criticism, the history of traditions, the history of exegesis, church history, the history of theology, the history of popular devotion and the history of research: all to demonstrate the "complete historicity of Christianity".[8]

But the modern science of history is itself full of doubts about its methods, and is asking serious questions about its ability to form theories.[9] It is generally known and the process has been

[6] Danto, op. cit., p. iii. Jean Bodin, Methodus ad facilem historiarum cognitionem (Amsterdam, 1650; reprint Aalen, 1967), chap. I, p. 8.
[7] H. Peukert, in J. B. Metz and T. Rendtorff (ed.), Die Theologie in der interdisciplinären Forschung (Düsseldorf, 1971), p. 68.
[8] U. Wilckens, in Metz and Rendtorff, op. cit., p. 85.
[9] Cf. R. Koselleck and W.-D. Stempel (ed.), Geschichten und Geschichte (Munich, 1972).

exhaustively described and documented by Reinhard Koselleck, how the (more or less true) stories of the early historiographers became the collective singular of history (*historia ipsa*), and how as a result of the equivocation between history as teller and history as told every possible hypostasis takes the place of the narrator which historians have rushed to give up.[10] Modern historians do all they can in order to have to tell as few stories as possible. "This is not a story" (Diderot) or "No more stories" (Michael Scharang) would be suitable titles for many situations in which historians practise their profession. Golo Mann's vast historical tale of *Wallenstein* (Frankfurt, 1971) is the sublime and possibly the last exception which confirms our rule.

If it is true that storytelling is despised by scientific students of history, we have to ask whether there is any place at all in modern society where it remains unquestioned. Walter Benjamin and Theodor Adorno say no, and have diagnosed the end of storytelling as a general condition. [11] Nevertheless the novel still exists as a literary form and retains a strong (though not expanding) position on the book market. And "This is not a story" and "No more stories" are in the end titles of stories. I would describe the position in the terms used by the critic Reinhart Baumgart, that there still exists today an extensive narrative literature, but that this form of literature is characterized by a style in which storytelling itself is brought into the story.[12] This means that when writers writing at present tell a story they subject the process of storytelling itself to critical examination and make this examination in turn part of their story. Naïve storytelling can be found today almost only in trivial literature. Even the literature of fiction has also clearly lost its narrative innocence and confirms our thesis that this society has, perhaps finally, adopted post-narrative habits of communication.

And now to conclusions. It is impossible simply to nullify

[10] Reinhard Koselleck, "Historia magistra vitae", in *Natur und Geschichte. Karl Löwith zum 70. Geburtstag* (Stuttgart, 1967), pp. 196–219.

[11] W. Benjamin, *Illuminations* (New York, 1968; London, 1970); Th. W. Adorno, *Noten zur Literatur* (Frankfurt, 1965), vol. I, p. 63.

[12] R. Baumgart, *Literatur für Zeitgenossen* (Frankfurt, 1966, 2nd edn., 1970); *id., Aussichten des Romans oder Hat Literatur Zukunft?* (Neuwied, 1968).

the holy or unholy alliance between theology and the sciences, especially the science of history. A merely narrative theology is now hardly conceivable, especially in our post-narrative age. But the criticism of theology, both inside and outside theology proper, may nevertheless be allowed to question the unquestioning acceptance of this old covenant with history. There is no particularly obvious reason why theologians should share the historians' fixation on the truth of a story. A factual basis is not a necessary condition for a story to say something to us or move us. Fictional stories can also produce this effect. It is a category of narrative in general and not specific to history, and a made-up story can do just as much as a story about actual events to produce in its hearers that further action and retelling which is the task of those who want to go and do likewise. Doctrine is not an unavoidable stage in this journey, and may even be a diversion, when one considers that narrative and practical ("political") theology are both concerned with actions. This is not to say that theology will be able to become to such an extent a practical discipline that it can withdraw from the alliance with the theoretical disciplines. Even as a theoretical discipline, however, it does not need, through lack of faith, to deny its traditional stories. A theory of stories would be a wide-ranging programme for such a discipline.[13] With its help theology could also offer assistance to various other disciplines, including history, which have themselves so far shown little interest in the rules governing the stories in their own fields. Nor would this research programme coincide with the familiar methods of form criticism. One important distinction would be that in this theory of stories the fundamental discrimination in academic circles against stories in favour of discursive argument would be regarded as a negative quality. Even a consistent theory of stories would on

[13] Suggestions for such a programme are to be found in the most recent work of literary structuralism, where it is not involved in what Alfred Schmidt has called "the latest attack on history". Cf. Roland Barthes, "Introduction à l'analyse structurale des récits", *Communications*, 8 (1966), pp. 1–27; Tzvetan Todorov, *Poétique de la Prose* (Paris, 1971); Karlheinz Stierle, "L'histoire comme exemple, l'exemple comme histoire", *Poétique*, 10 (1972), pp. 176–98. Volume 18 (1972) of *Communications* is devoted to "L'Evénement" and contains interesting contributions on the place of stories in history.

this view necessarily prove inadequate in the face of a simple pre-told or retold story which produced an effect on its hearers which made them "doers of the word" and retellers in their turn. If pastoral theology knows such stories, it has chosen the better part. Giuseppe Roncalli knew this intuitively, as he showed when he greeted a group of Jewish visitors with the words, "I am your brother Joseph". That was the retelling of a story which he, the twenty-third Bishop of Rome named John, shared with his Jewish brothers from Israel. The effect of a story on that day recreated a very old storytelling community.

Translated by Francis McDonagh

Jean-Pierre Jossua

Christian Experience and Communicating the Faith

I. The Present State of Christian Witness

SEVERAL articles in this issue analyse the contemporary crisis in
the Christian witness. There can be no doubt that this crisis is
intensified by another which affects the very consciousness of
faith. This interdependence is not simply psycho-sociological,
resulting from the effect on the mentality of a group of its progressive cultural isolation within society at large, which absorbs
the members of that group but does not accept their particular
message. It is in the first instance theological: faith *is* in the
measure that it is articulated. Any devaluation of its language
results in a confusion as to how it should be interpreted; every
barrier to its communication raises the question of its universal
efficacy for salvation. This has given rise to a serious situation
which some evade by overstressing the practical, here-and-now
aspect of Christianity, and which many others refuse to acknowledge, taking refuge behind a "missionary" vocabulary which has
lost more or less all its relevance.

One thing is certain—the Church's official or prevailing
ideology has never been so "missionary", particularly in France.
Born of the simultaneous discovery of the actual extent of un-
belief, and of the good faith of those who have never really
understood the gospel message, the vocabulary of "evangeliza-
tion" has enjoyed considerable vogue since the war. It made it
possible to determine the scope of "Catholic action" movements,
which were henceforth to leave all "temporal activity" to the

personal responsibility of their members. In this way were resolved the ambiguities as to the Christian character of these movements which had attended their origins, but always at the risk of leaving them with an abstract objective, divorced from all human reality. This vocabulary has enhanced with the prestige of "the mission" all enterprises concerned with the inner renewal of the Christian community: catechetical, liturgical, sacramental. It has given a new orientation and the responsibility for providing alternatives to a clergy unhappily engulfed in the crisis caused by a style of ministry whose ideals, social expressions, and even concrete functions were rapidly becoming meaningless. The considerable difficulties with which this missionary endeavour was forced to contend—the want of recognizable signs and above all the existence of counter-witnesses—could not pass unnoticed, but in general it all boiled down to a test of credibility for the Church. Though this factor cannot, of course, be denied, and though it continues to bear considerable weight, it can be safely argued that the evolution of the Church since Vatican II justifies one in drawing the conclusion that it is far from being isolated, and that even when such preliminary obstacles have been removed, the problem remains intact.

The contrast, in fact, between this ideology and the reality is startling—Christian witness has reached a state of virtually total deadlock. In recent years, the various reasons for this have been set out so frequently that there could be no excuse for reintroducing them here, except in the form of a mere enumeration. In the first place, then, there is the collapse, or at least quasi-total inadequacy, of the old ways of approaching the God of Jesus Christ. Thus the religious quest inspires only the few. Philosophy, as practised by philosophers, does not lead finally to this question. The apologetics of values, whose inner dynamics should point to God, succeed in convincing only believers. The canonization of secular concerns, which permits some people to discern the omnipresence of religion, opens out to everything except Christianity. The "absolute demands" of the historical process are called in question by the failure of the philosophies of history, while some critics tend to discredit anything savouring of the existential, the interior or the personal. Revivals of religiosity, all of them curiously ambiguous in character, last as long as any other fashion. Secondly, there is everything that comes as a result of the historical adaptation of Christianity—regional variations in its basic needs, linguistic anachronisms in its dogmatic and theological formulations, the dependence of its liturgy, customs and law on cultural factors.

To put it more plainly, the language of "mysteries" is not a fit vehicle for communication with non-believers—the ancient Church realized this, but the quibblings of a dying "Christendom" have managed to ignore it. On the other hand, the "language of proclamation" is itself very circumscribed culturally, to the extent of being a language for the initiated, which was not the case in the Jewish world, or even completely in the Greek. At all events, it cannot normally afford to economize on methods of approach, and always presupposes a certain breadth of discourse, a looking forward to the future. In the third place, we are all well aware that the most deep-seated problem is, in fact, that which underlies the first, mentioned above: in our present civilization, neither abundance nor emptiness, neither meaningfulness nor the lack of it, neither peaceful fulfilment nor revolution, constitute, from the outset, a basis for understanding, a disposition, a summons, a signpost pointing to faith.

Finally, if this aspect of the problem has attracted a good deal of attention, there is a fourth which, although continuously in evidence, has been little enough examined by Christians. The individuals or groups they meet, and for whom they wish to exercise their responsibility as witnesses to the gospel, are not pagans. If the "missionary" vocabulary has had the advantage of being able to state openly that they are non-believers, it has had the corresponding disadvantage of equating them with the non-evangelized. They are rather post-Christians—their outlook is influenced by the fact that they consider themselves, either in the course of their own development or in the history of their culture, to have transcended Christianity. They place themselves beyond it, whether this be to criticize and reject it, or to reinterpret it within the framework of an "adult" and post-religious humanism, or even of a "universal religion". Such are the unforeseen obstacles which the inherent demands of witness place in its way! It is indeed difficult to become a Christian today!

And yet it is possible to be one, to live as such, without ceasing to belong to this very world, in the midst of which the journey towards faith tends to become impracticable. We are not concerned, here, with trying to discover how it can be done, can, that is, in the sense of a radical possibility whose affirmation is precisely the act of faith itself! But we must inquire whether one can believe humanly speaking, and whether communication among believers is possible—both justifications for belief, which would provide faith with its human foundation. With the breakdown of the classical *preambula fidei*, which had served simultaneously as avenues of approach and as exterior supports to credibility, what becomes of that certain proof which the mind demands? More often than not, it seems to me, real proof, the motive for belief which rationally justifies faith, is to be found within faith itself. It is the manifold richness of human experience which, by its very fruitfulness, bears witness to the subject, whenever he succeeds in apprehending it, that he is not being deluded—in spite of the fact that he stands, in virtue of his choice, outside the possibility of a certainty founded entirely on proofs. It is this experience which, in rising above the established proofs, demonstrates to him, in practice, that it can survive the attacks of criticism. It is this same experience that Christians communicate to one another by means of symbols, as they repeat the age-old words of the message, which then comes to life for them. And so it is possible for a Christian to be and to declare himself Christian today. He has not always managed, however, to step outside the charmed circle of this original experience and stereotyped language. And if one does not find oneself there from the beginning, how does one get in? Must one plunge in with one's feet tied? Maybe, but all the same there is here one thread of which we must not let go.

In order to follow it up, it would seem indispensable to begin with a criticism of the missionary-type ideology and recruitment attributed to Christians. These hide the seriousness of the state of non-communication which is the essential feature of the present crisis of witness. They place the man who bears witness in a disturbingly false position when it comes to presenting the faith. In reality, he never acts in his own right; he stands poised between the gratuitousness of an unforeseeable call and the unsearchable freedom of the response made, both unobtrusive, and the latter hidden, perhaps, from the eyes of the speaker himself. They lead to a militant approach, lacking in human content and spiritual depth, whereas it is important, above all, to exist, personally and collectively, as men who move in this world, and yet carry on a dialogue with their God. They imply an ecclesiological schema for Church-World relations which has been thought out in terms of externalization and dialogue, and so exposes the currently alienated state of the clerics who have drawn it up. The only possible starting-point will be discovered, in fact, by a kind of turning round and back. We must no longer set out from a ready-made language, but from human life, as it is lived by Christians in the light of the gospel and becomes that Christian experience which carries within it its own means of verification. There will then be some likelihood of our discovering a language through which Christians and non-Christians can meet one another and a way of approach to faith be opened up.

II. From Christian Life to Experience and Speech

1. Clarifying the Meaning of Christian Experience

If human existence is normally accompanied by an attendant self-awareness which grasps its significance, in part at least, the term experience may be charged with a further meaning. It refers, then, to an event or series of events, in so far as they are recognized, in retrospect, as meaningful by one or several individuals who have been involved in them.[1] Inevitably, this shift of emphasis, which will be analysed in more detail shortly, implies, with respect to the reality of existence, a kind of double

[1] For a discussion of the various meanings attached to the term *experience*, with reflection on the attendant ambiguities and inevitable philosophical implications of its use, I would refer to the critical note which features at the end of a collection of essays, *Une foi exposée*, to which I refer below in note 8. See also: J. Mouroux, "L'expérience chrétienne", *Théologie*, 26 (Paris, 1954), which is now out of date, but served as a very powerful catalyst; M. Demaison, "L'expérience de la foi, épreuve du croyant", *Lumière et Vie*, 19 (1970), pp. 39–58.

setback of which it is very important not to lose sight. First of all, an impoverishment, since not everything that is genuinely experienced can come within the grasp of our understanding, at any rate at a given moment. And then a measure of obscurity, for to a great extent consciousness is not transparent, even to itself: it can be misled by anything which only reaches it in a disguised form, its most basic structures are not the object of direct apprehension.[2] This does not diminish the decisive value which the possibility of grasping and understanding his own existence has for man. Indeed, everyone recognizes the importance which the notion of "retrospect" has acquired today in philosophy and the human sciences.

Taken in this interpretative sense, the term experience may be defined with reference to five mutually complementary characteristics. (a) There is experience whenever there is insight into our relationship with ourselves, others, to the world and God: this insight is always the reflection, in a subject capable of understanding it, of a situation or event in which he finds himself caught up. (b) Any mention of experience indicates that there has been a true participation of the subject in the event, even if such participation is not always actual in the more obvious sense and can be described as a cultural sharing full of meaning. (c) Material participation, on the other hand, is not enough, and subjective *awareness*—the motion of separation, of mentally standing back from oneself—is a decisive element, as we suggested at the beginning. (d) Next, such growth of awareness in a human mind is accompanied by *interpretation*, rational explanation of what has been grasped intuitively. (e) Finally, the term experience almost always connotes something *all-embracing*, and refers to the perception as thought out and unified by the interpretation of an entire area of existence (affective, intellectual or aesthetic experience) or of history.

To speak of Christian experience, then, is to point to a co-

---

[2] A. Vergote, in a remarkable passage, "Dimensions anthropologiques de l'eucharistie", in *L'eucharistie, symbole et realité* (Gembloux and Paris, 1970), exposes the dangers of exclusive insistence on spontaneous experience when it is set up as the only standard of judgment. He bases his argument as much on a nascent suspicion of studies of anthropological structures as on a vindication of the structures of grace as normative.

ordinated corpus of individual experiences as these have been lived, reflected on and interpreted by believers. For every Christian they are of unquestionable personal significance. For each one of us, they constitute an ensemble whose inner coherence is revealed or imposed by the interpretation. Furthermore, if they are proper to the individual they are likewise common to many; they are not, strictly speaking, unique, either as such, or in the context of faith, which points them out and unifies them. We expect to undergo the same experiences. Finally, they are also communal in one other respect: Christian experience is, in the first place, collective, social and historical; the category of experience never implies limitation to the individual, the strictly personal, even when lived in the same way by a large number.

Christians witness, in fact, to an experience which is complex, made up of elements of conviction, action, encounter, satisfaction and specific trials. It is personal and collective at the same time. It is lived out in different ways by believers, and yet they recognize among themselves certain common factors. It is many-sided, and develops from tensions that exist between factors whose theoretical unity according to the message in no way guarantees immediate compatibility in fact. And yet it does admit of real unity —faith binds together the sum total of those individual experiences by interpreting them, gathering them into a single perspective, and articulating them in depth.[3]

This experience can be put into words, it can yield to language and become speech. But that new threshold will not be crossed without a further shedding of superfluous weight, similar to that to which I referred when discussing the passage from existence to experience. Description and itemization will never exhaust the richness of lived experience, even in so far as this is conscious. Symbolic language itself, which can go so much further than rational speech, will not suggest everything. Besides, if the mystery of God's presence is not entirely within the realm of the experience already, it can only become so in a very particular way

[3] For a typical example, taken from experience, see "La foi comme dépassement de la tension entre l'action et la prière", *Revue des Sciences philosophiques et théologiques*, 56 (1972), and P. Jaquemont, "Is Action Prayer?", *Concilium*, Nov. 1972 (American Edn., vol. 79).

which will impose its own conditions on the mode of expression. Thus experience lived in faith and confronting the mystery can apprehend itself, test the validity of its apprehension, and ultimately achieve self-expression. But it cannot apprehend, or verify, or express that of which it is experience in the most radical sense, vestiges of which can be discerned in it only negatively—the presence of the Absent, silence beyond words. Very often speech will just have to point to the existence of unchartered tracts which remain unexpressed. Once these limitations have been recorded, however, it will remain true that communication is not impossible, and we must now evaluate the significance of this fact.

2. *Christian Experience and the Profession of Faith*

Christian experience is the primordial interpretation expressed in action, the realization, in the life of believers today, of that mystery of salvation which the creed proclaims. On the other hand, the profession of faith, now as at the beginning, is always the reduction to credal formulae of a lived reality rich with meaning. If one considers the first professions of faith, even those which we recognize as the Word of God, they already appear as the verbal expression of a lived experience of salvation which is, in this case, the basic event and the communal experience of salvation. These two poles—the resurrection of Jesus and the Church of Pentecost—are distinguished but inseparable: the one cannot be studied objectively apart from the other, but neither can the specific characteristics of each be glossed over. Still today, Christian experience, far from being subjective, leads us to a realm beyond the distinction between subject and object, to the very reality of the salvation which is there being worked out, and which is at one and the same time our own work and the act of him who saves us.

The content of the profession of faith is Jesus Christ. Jesus discovered in his mission: the prophet who inaugurates for men a history of liberty and love in the world, and the master of the knowledge of God enabling us to seek him in truth and live in his presence. Jesus Christ recognized in his mystery: the paradox of transcendence risked and given up for our salvation in the historical and human dimension. Not God clothed in humanity, not even God *and* man; but God *as* man,[4] God revealed and surrendering himself with a freedom and in a destiny like ours. To this identification of Jesus Christ there corresponds a decisive factor intrinsic to faith, and intrinsic also to the totality of Christian existence and experience.[5] Fundamentally, it is the paradox of an unconditional human commitment to this self-commitment of God in Jesus Christ, of an absolute risk. In effect it is a creative act which rediscovers the true features of the Saviour's life and mission: his simultaneous search for, expectation of and openness to that mysterious Other he called his father, together with his passion for freedom, his assurance that love, the service of others in history, is possible.

If in Jesus Christ the totally transcendent is revealed through the totally human (and not the superhuman!), if God is present in the life of a man, and if Christian experience—participation in this mystery, lived interpretation of this belief—is in its turn built up, according to the same pattern, on the same regime of God's gifts, we need to renew our approach quite as much to the experience as to the mystery of Christ. Just as christology had to move beyond that attempt to take seriously once more the humanity of Christ, which characterized theology at the beginning of the century, so we must do more than simply take seriously the humanity of the Christian, in reaction against all forms of angelism. Must we not say that the place where the most mysterious aspects of the new life in Christ are made concrete— the personal encounter with God and the witness we bear him—

[4] On this basic orientation of contemporary christology, which links Scripture with the most ancient tradition of the Church, see K. Rahner, "Problèmes actuels de christologie", *Ecrits théologiques* (Paris, 1959), and "Réflexions théologiques sur l'Incarnation", *Ecrits théologiques*, 3 (Paris, 1962), pp. 81–101; W. Pannenberg, *Esquisse d'une christologie* (French translation: Paris, 1971); C. Duquoc, *Christologie, essai dogmatique*, 2 vols. (Paris, 1968 and 1972).

[5] The dependence of the entire Christian economy on our identification with Christ, to which there corresponds an inner determination of faith (which is no neutral force) and therefore an obligatory definition of the confession of faith, ensures that the question of a rule of faith can be posed in a real, and not merely extrinsic, way. See my article "Rule of Faith and Orthodoxy", *Concilium*, Jan. 1970 (American Edn., vol. 51) and, more recently, on the confession of faith and its relation to experience and to the rule of faith: "Signification des confessions de foi", *Istina*, 17 (1972), pp. 48–56.

must be the human existence and experience of the Christian, and not some superhuman, unfamiliar or miraculous dimension. And is this not an affirmation that nothing divine has a place in our experience which comes there otherwise than through the mediation of the human? Certainly, this humanness, which is fundamental—and in the last analysis a paradox—for Christian experience, presupposes that open-ended approach to humanity implied in the ancient Jewish and Christian phrase, "the image of God"— which is essentially fashioned in the likeness of its prototype. The ancient Christian concept of man was able to acknowledge both his finiteness and his openness to what would later be known as the "supernatural", which is not a thing received, but a loving relationship, capable of changing his entire life.[6]

3. The Pathway of Experience

This elucidation of the concept of Christian experience and the attempt at theological interpretation had as their twofold aim to set out a pathway, a route along which Christian witness might move, and a mode of expression that would make dialogue possible. If the Christian experience can still be lived out in today's world as a precious grace, and yet the pathways leading to it appear to be blocked, there remains the possibility of living among men within the framework of a particular way of personal and communal life. If this is of genuine worth, it will lead them to inquire about it, and then about the expectation on which it is founded. From the power of the gospel to bear fruit in the simplest and most ordinary daily life, on to the most particular and mysterious aspects of the life of faith, from one human experience to another, a pathway can be traced whose authenticity is attested from within the experience itself, and language will be able, in retrospect, to interpret the meaning.

I am not concerned here to describe this pathway in detail, but I should like to indicate a little better its actual course, and so reveal the analogical character which, at the various stages, the affirmation of its essential humanity assumes. To begin with, there

---

[6] See the bibliographical references in "L'enjeu de la recherche théologique actuelle sur le Salut", *Revue des Sciences philosophiques et théologiques*, 54 (1970), p. 33, n. 14 and p. 36, nn. 17 and 18.

is a certain Christian way of living through the experiences, trials and searchings common to all men, a Christian sense of life. It matters little that this sense is not the *specific* preserve of believers, it matters little that the choices it involves, from among the multiplicity of human options, can coincide with those that will be made by other men. It remains a fact that, in the many ways it has of confronting the demands of existence, the gospel is never neutral. The characteristically Christian choices are characteristically human choices and show forth, in their individual and collective existence, not a physiognomy that can be differentiated in any way, but rather an understanding of life, which is offered to all those who search.[7] The practice of the beatitudes, of compassion for all suffering, and of love towards one's enemies surely point to a human existence which is stretching itself to its own limits, at the same time as they give human expression to the life of Christ in us.

Behind these choices, there is a more radical choice which gives them their basic orientation; beyond the hope of realizing them in history there is a further hope which draws us onwards. If, in the life of a Christian, nothing is changed—the taste of the earth and of time, daily joys and sorrows, dreams of make-believe and of art, happiness in friendship and in love, shared struggles that make men brothers, suffering, bereavement, sickness, death —and yet everything is changed, shot through with new meaning, this is because one additional factor runs through them all.

If, to divided mankind, a rallying-point of unity is offered, this is because a single basic orientation binds all their experience together. Thus faith makes its presence felt in the winding ways of human existence, where it plays a crucial role, the foundation questioned by the man who has learned to recognize its fruits.

But although it involves unforeseen changes of position, and is directed towards a realm beyond experience, this very faith

[7] In anthropology, ethics or politics, even when it does not admit of *one* Christian anthropological, ethical or political schema, the gospel is not neutral. I have no intention of settling here the question of "universal" or secular ethics. But whether one should not think of it except as a goal ever in view but never reached, whether it fails to account, in the rigour of its rationalism, for the actual nature of human motives, or else makes room for "styles", for preferential scales of value, in any case it does not make an exhaustive analysis of the moral life of man.

appears, from the start, as a task, a risk, a conviction, an acceptance, representative of authentically human attitudes, comparable
to them, and susceptible of various interpretations. The testimony
it bears is unquestionably paradoxical, but is it any the less human
for all that in its method of communication, inquiry, dialogue,
acceptance or rejection?

Step by step, in one experience after another, one discovers the
Church as a community, a house, a school, a people pregnant with
the mystery of communion. For is it not in words borrowed from
our life, consigned to a book, and passed on through the experience and reflection of earlier generations, that we sense the
presence of a Word? Is it not through the simple gestures of the
sacraments, sometimes taken from daily life, sometimes trans-
figured by festal joy, that God allows himself to be "touched" in
the symbol? And is not prayer itself like love, a quite simple
experience in which presence and absence, peace and fear of
abandonment, are mingled?

4. *The Chances for Communication*

Can we now take one further step: that which leads on from
this experience to speech? The answer is that we must, in fact,
set out on a slightly different route from the one followed by the
approach of faith. We live among non-believing friends, and the
desire for mutual understanding is interpreted by us all as a need,
as a human duty. In whatever way we interpret the different
solutions offered by this man or that for the basic problems of
existence, we are able to recognize them all as aspects of the
human, of which it is essential that others too should have
knowledge and understanding. This search and this exchange
are the essence of humanity. When our friends describe their way
of understanding and working out their destiny, they expect us
to understand them, and this, I think, is, in effect, what happens.
On the other hand, their friendship and their esteem are per-
plexed by our faith, which remains foreign to them. If, in order
to clarify things for them, we speak of it in the language of the
creed, their perplexity is merely increased. Could we not, then,
speak to them, instead, of that which we live, of our experience?
If, as we have asserted, it is so thoroughly human, why should it

be humanly inexpressible? Even if the symbol—though not that which presupposes initiation—often stops short at description, and the mystery which surrounds it is only manifest through the vestiges it leaves there, and even though silence must sometimes point out the place of those intimations that cannot be expressed in words, could we not, with no other motive than the exchange itself, explain to them in a universal language why our Christian experience is so precious to us?[8]

That is also, in its own sense, an act of witness, at the meeting of ways. But it is to be distinguished by its very intention of opening up a possible avenue of approach for those we wish to invite to faith. Caught between these two aims, there emerges the contemporary hesitation of Christians in the matter of witness. This hesitation makes the proclamation that should be salvific timid instead, and renders suspect a dialogue which thoughtlessly imposes its own terms. In a certain sense, however, that question goes beyond the problem I set out to consider in this article. With the missionary ideology in a weakened or withered state and witness in a state of deadlock, I simply wished to point out that fidelity to experience does not merely offer to the Christian of today the possibility of living his faith in all its vigour, but also the chance of opening up a way to others who are searching for the gospel, and perhaps of developing a way of speaking which our contemporaries can understand.

Translated by Sarah Fawcett

---

[8] With P. Jaquemont and B. Quelquejeu I have attempted to realize this ambition in *Une foi exposée* (Paris, 1972).

Robert Spaemann

Mysticism and Enlightenment

I. WITTGENSTEIN'S TREATMENT OF MYSTICISM IN THE "TRACTATUS"

THE famous proposition with which Wittgenstein concluded his *Tractatus Logico-philosophicus*[1]—"what we cannot speak about we must consign to silence"—has become the slogan of neo-positivism. Wittgenstein's own attitude to the ineffable was no different from that of many mystics who said that their spiritual experiences were beyond description and then proceeded to talk about them. "There are, indeed," Wittgenstein states a few propositions earlier, "things that cannot be put into words. They *make themselves manifest*. They are what is mystical" (6.522). The concept of mysticism occurs frequently in Wittgenstein's writings: "It is not *how* things are in the world that is mystical, but *that* it exists" (6.44). And: "To view the world *sub specie aeterni* is to view it as a whole—a limited whole. Feeling the world as a limited whole—it is this that is mystical" (6.45).

Calling on his own experience, Wittgenstein once described in a lecture on ethics two feelings that are of the type depicted in the *Tractatus* as mystical. First of all the feeling of amazement that anything should exist at all. And then the feeling of absolute security, of a type that is beyond the reach of changing circumstances. Wittgenstein at once added that to express such feelings could only lead to absurdity. Why? Because the feeling would

---

[1] *Tractatus Logico-Philosophicus*, translated by D. F. Pears and B. F. McGuinness (London and New York, 1961).

have to be expressed through propositions that obtained in all circumstances, tautological propositions that have no truth-conditions. There is no circumstance that renders false the proposition that something exists. For if there were nothing the proposition that declared there was something would not be false but instead would be nothing at all. And the proposition I am safe, the meaning of my existence is indestructible, cannot in any state of affairs be shown to be false if it is expressing an authentic experience. For the experience, the feeling, to which Wittgenstein refers indicates precisely the independence of all possible data. Propositions that have no truth-conditions Wittgenstein calls obviously meaningless. For a proposition is the expression of its truth-condition. It cannot express unconditional "conditionless truth".

Even so, there is such a thing as the experience of the unconditional. Wittgenstein calls such an experience mystical. He speaks of people for whom after long-standing doubts the meaning of life has become clear and who were then unable to say what this meaning was. The meaning cannot be expressed. It *shows* itself. That is mystical that shows itself. It does so in language and precisely for this reason cannot be expressed through language. "What *can* be shown, *cannot* be said" (4.1212). In so far as philosophy separates what can be said from what can be thought one is able to discern within the resultant distinction what cannot be said and what cannot be thought. "It will signify what cannot be said, by presenting clearly what can be said" (4.115). What cannot be said Wittgenstein also calls transcendental. It is that which shows itself in saying what can be said. Hegel also, incidentally, held that propositions could not express our experience of an experience—in this context Hegel referred to "the speculative" and Wittgenstein to "what is higher". But if Hegel considered that the speculative could nevertheless be expressed then this was because for him language was more than the totality of all basic propositions. Wittgenstein, on the other hand, held that all reflexive speech was meaningless, while maintaining that such meaninglessness was necessary if the world was to be seen correctly. Even the proposition concerning the meaninglessness of reflexive propositions belongs to the class of meaningless propositions. It says nothing. It is simply a handling instruction which can only be understood by implementing it.

In Wittgenstein's later pragmatic theory of language games the contrast between representing and meaning is completely abandoned. But neither in this later theory is there anything about mysticism, since the feeling of the world as a limited whole no longer has the contrapuntal significance that it had in the *Tractatus*. The thesis that the sense of the world, that which the world does not accidentally permit to be, must lie outside the world (6.41), is related to the other thesis in the *Tractatus* that all propositions are of equal value and can express nothing of what is higher (6.42).

Ethics, for example, is what is higher. The *Tractatus* describes it as transcendental, and in a journal entry for 1916 Wittgenstein called it a condition of the world that as such cannot be expressed in propositions but instead is "profoundly mysterious".[2] But in the ethical writings of the analytical school and their reference to the later *Philosophical Investigations*, ethics is grouped with the class of language games. It ceases to be based upon an ineffable mystical experience. The *Philosophical Investigations* also places prayer among the class of language games and in so doing encourages the development of an analytical philosophy of religion. But it seems to me that this philosophy is less a reflection of original experience than of Wittgenstein's earlier discussion of mysticism.

Wittgenstein's discussion of mysticism was conducted without any close familiarity with the mystical traditions of East or West. Neither does it seem to have been a consequence of a spiritual journey such as the great mystics often experienced. On the other hand, it cannot be said of his discussion of this subject that it lacks originality, or that it is merely metaphorical, for it describes an experience not unlike that described by Plotinus, Meister Eckhart, Ruysbroeck or John of the Cross. There *are* things that cannot be put into words, not as the result of a syllogism, but as making themselves manifest, as cause, not in the sense of causality, but as a property that suggests a meaning that lies beyond this, of what can be said outside the world. This meaning shows itself as a medium of absolute security, without thereby excluding states of affairs that could be to our disadvantage. The

[2] *Schriften*, I (Frankfurt, 1969), p. 171.

concept of *resignatio in infernum* has been familiar to Western mysticism since Ruysbroeck. Harmony with God's will reaches its zenith in the readiness to assent to eternal separation from him, should that be his will. In other words, the state of mystical security achieves its highest affirmation in the rejection of any religion-conditioned view of the future which, as it always relates to the individual, would itself be a ceaseless state of affairs. Unsurpassable union with a cause, interpreted in Western mysticism as union with the will of God, is such that it makes the distinction between the here and the beyond, the present and the future, disappear. Heaven is no longer seen as future reward for present constancy but is itself identical, as absolute present, with such constancy: *nunc stans*. Fénelon, one of mysticism's foremost interpreters, wrote: "To enclose oneself in the present moment is one of the most important rules of the spiritual life."[3] And J. P. de Caussade speaks of "the sacrament of the present moment".[4]

Here, Wittgenstein's comments are again relevant: "If we take eternity to mean not infinite temporal duration but timelessness, then eternal life belongs to those who live in the present. . . . Not only is there no guarantee of the temporal immortality of the soul, that is to say of its eternal survival after death; but in any case, this assumption completely fails to accomplish the purpose for which it has always been intended. Or is some riddle solved by my surviving for ever? Is not this eternal life itself as much of a riddle as our present life? The solution of the riddle of life in space and time lies *outside* space and time" (6.4312). Blessedness is not a consequence of the virtuous life, as it was for Kant, but, as for Spinoza and Fichte, it is the virtuous life itself, and that means life in the present. "He who lives in the present lives without fear and without hope."[5] The banishing of fear and hope was precisely what the mystics were so often accused of. Madame Guyon wrote: "Through losing hope one recovers peace. Love without trust or mistrust is the sole guarantee of eternity."

[3] Fénelon, *Œuvres complètes*, VIII, p. 11.
[4] *L'Abandon à la divine providence.*
[5] *Tagebücher, Werke*, I, p. 169.

II. The Complementary Function of the Mystical in Wittgenstein's Programme of Enlightenment

I do not want to go deeper into the question of Wittgenstein's mysticism because what concerns me here is the relationship in his writings between mysticism and the tendency towards radical enlightenment. In describing the Wittgenstein of the *Tractatus* as a philosopher of the Enlightenment, I am not thinking of the classical Kantian definition of enlightenment—the use of unaided reason—since, in our times, this description has become as trivial a postulate as it is a problematic reality. It is questioned openly only when a political movement sets itself up as an implementation of enlightenment and where to this end one particular party attempts to lay down limits to thinking for oneself. But this happens precisely to expedite the inner purpose of the Enlightenment and this purpose is the homogenization of experience; the total objectivization of reality by means of its progressive conversion into a complex of structural quantitative relationships; and through these means the unlimited expansion of the extent to which all things can be controlled and manoeuvred.

So far this tendency has found its most important expression in the philosophical writings that have taken their inspiration from Wittgenstein's *Tractatus*. "Whatever can be said can be said clearly; and what we cannot speak about we must consign to silence." In this proposition Wittgenstein summarized the purpose of his book, which was to bring the limits of thought and speech and the limits of objectivization into alignment. A rule of language is introduced that excludes as an object of possible questioning whatever is not the ultimate state of affairs. "*The riddle* does not exist" (6.5). For Kant, metaphysical questions were as unavoidable as they were unanswerable. Wittgenstein wrote: "When the answer cannot be put into words, neither can the question be put into words" (6.5). The objective of enlightenment is the removal of all religious, ethical and aesthetic inhibitions that are in opposition to the total transference of the world to the "totality of facts". "The world is all that is the case", begins the *Tractatus*. And towards the end we read: "All propositions are of equal value" (6.4). "In the world everything is as it is, and everything happens as it does happen: *in* it no

value exists—and if it did exist, it would have no value" (6.41).
The meaning of this becomes a lot clearer when we consider the
way in which sociology and psychology regard values—namely,
as sociological or psychological facts, and thus precisely not as
values. Heidegger has already designated the concept of value as
the mysterious dissolution of whatever is thereby intended, as
the herald of nihilism.

We can now see that for Wittgenstein mysticism is exactly
complementary to this understanding of enlightenment. "The
drive towards the mystical comes from the inability of science to
satisfy our needs",[6] says Wittgenstein in a journal entry. And in
the *Tractatus*: "We feel that when *all possible* scientific questions have been answered, the problems of life remain completely
untouched" (6.52). Such language might have come straight from
a sermon. Why Wittgenstein speaks of the drive towards mysticism and not towards religion can be seen in the conclusion of
this proposition: "Of course there are then no questions left, and
this itself is the answer" (6.52). That is to say that the problems
of life that remain completely untouched by the findings of science
do not for that reason become the objects of renewed thematic
investigations or of practical efforts on one's own part but just
disappear altogether through the answering of the scientific questions. This is a typical mystical paradox. But there is no room
in Wittgenstein's theory of language for paradox as the legitimate
means of speaking about the experience of meaning, and yet it is
precisely paradox that shows through in what he does. He speaks
paradoxically of what cannot be said. Thus, when he writes: "To
believe in God means to believe that the facts of the world are not
yet disposed of."[7] Or, "God does not reveal himself *in* the world"
(6.432). But then: "How everything comports itself is God. God
is how everything comports itself."[8] In other words, God is not
the many; he is outside the many, but he is not at the same time
the other as against the many. From Parmenides to Hegel, metaphysics has sought to ponder this relationship. We see here an
appeal to an experience, critical of metaphysics, that precedes
and underlies all metaphysics and that has even been quite frequently hidden from it. But it was Wittgenstein's conviction that

[6] *Schriften*, I, p. 142.   [7] *Schriften*, I, p. 167.   [8] *Schriften*, I, p. 171.

it is the exhaustive presentation of what can scientifically be said that brings what cannot be said to light.

III. The Theme of Illumination as Index of the Debate between Enlightenment and Mysticism

These references to mysticism in connection with Wittgenstein are intended neither to further the interpretation of his writings nor to provide deeper insights into the nature of mysticism. Such benefits could hardly be expected anyway for Wittgenstein's understanding of mysticism remains somewhat vague and what he says about the "feeling" of the mystical is largely uncritical. The great mystics have always described the condition of mystical union as the absence of particular feelings. Reference to Wittgenstein ought rather to throw light, through a somewhat extreme example, on the thesis that in an enlightened world the moment of mystical experience gains a decisive general significance. It is no accident that the era of the early Enlightenment in the seventeenth century is also the period that Bremond felt justified in describing as that of the "mystical invasion". It should be noted that this invasion occurred not as a counteraction to the Enlightenment but that in a particular sense it was identical with it.

Faced by the nominalist positivism of the orthodox attitude to revelation, the mystical movements of the sixteenth and seventeenth centuries sought through the return to an "inner light" the removal of the new subjectivity of the alternatives—emancipation seen on the one hand as relapse into the natural state and on the other as a heteronomous personal task. To the orthodox, the doctrine of the inner light was mere fanaticism because it relied upon a power that was beyond verification and that was directly communicated. The charge of fanaticism, a common matter at this time, was a denunciation of the return to direct inspiration. Yet where religion has lost the experience of immediacy it is itself condemned to fanaticism. Its communications —texts, Church, worship, prayers, and so on—remain as a whole a non-communicated and self-centred complex, reflecting a reality undifferentiated from that of the modern world. But precisely where it is not in a position to set up a relationship with the modern world it succumbs uncritically to its presuppositions.

The religious eudemonism of the seventeenth century, for instance that of Bossuet, is structurally indistinguishable from the worldly eudemonism of Helvetius. And Helvetius appealed ironically to this agreement with orthodoxy. As something uncommunicated, faith seen as orthodoxy, "Church faith" as Kant called it, is open to the charge of fanaticism. It rests upon external authorities. Attempts to argue rational authentication through miracles provokes incredulity: the miracle accounts themselves presuppose the faith they are intended to authenticate. Faith becomes a blind and irresponsible act of flight of the self from itself, or it presupposes some sort of immediate relationship between the subject, as self, and the object of faith. The Dutch and English sectarians called this an "inner light". Fénelon spoke of "inspiration" and the "inner word". "What would be the purpose", he asked, "of the external words of the pastor, or even of the Scriptures, if they did not communicate an inner word of the Holy Spirit which endowed the latter with its own effectiveness? The external word, even that of the Scriptures, would be an empty noise without the living and fruitful word of what is within. It is the letter alone that kills, and the spirit alone that enlivens."[9] David Hume adverted to the direct transition of the doctrine of the "inner light" to the Enlightenment and could therefore see the "fanaticism" of the mystics as something positive in contrast to the "superstitions" of the orthodox.

Fénelon, it is true, speaks characteristically of "inspiration", and the "inner word" and, renouncing the fanatical implication of the concept of illumination, he wrote: "Inspiration is without light."[10] The renunciation of the concept of illumination typifies French mysticism of the seventeenth century. Speaking of pure faith, Madame Guyon said that "it should be without evidence", thus opposing the Cartesian notion of self-conviction. The soul is "completely stripped of all certainty'·—a reversal of the Cartesian approach. But the obscurity of pure faith does not amount to obscurantism. Rather is it a rejection of everything in the world of religious perception that competes with rational evidence. The "dark night" of St John of the Cross, which he saw as a transitional stage on the way to mystical union, becomes the

[9] *Œuvres*, VI, p. 119.   [10] *Ibid*.

union itself. Likewise, Fénelon's anti-eudemonism, his doctrine of disinterested love, eliminates the opposed notion that stood in the way of the eudemonism of the Enlightenment. This is the only possible explanation of the enthusiasm shown for Fénelon by the Enlightenment, D'Alembert's composition on his behalf of a moving epigraph, and Rousseau's desire to become his lackey —all this in spite of the fact that they all saw his doctrine of pure love as a daydream. Yet it was precisely Fénelon's doctrine of pure love that enabled him in his reflections on the education of girls and in his *Télémaque*, the eighteenth century's most widely read book, to combine virtue and carefully controlled self-interest in a wholly unbiased way, whereas the religious eudemonism of the Jansenists led them to dig a deep educational rift between piety and temporal happiness.

It is mysticism that prevents religion from posturing as an other-worldly mirror image of the world. In the rule of Madame Guyon's *Association de l'Enfant Jésus* it states: "The child of grace is content with faith and with the act of surrender, travelling through these two the safest and most ordinary path, not striving for anything out of the usual such as pleasure, sweetness, pleasant sensations, sublime illumination, special gifts." And again: "The members of the Association shall not distinguish themselves from the children of the world in any way whatsoever, whether in clothing, habitation or ceremony of any sort. Such things have no significance in the Kingdom of Jesus. Instead, they will distinguish themselves through silence, Christian earnestness, composure, peace, gentleness, love, toleration of the neighbour, and through personal righteousness and integrity of life."[11] Fénelon quickly became the spiritual mentor of that strange, half-secret brotherhood which, in addition to pious society ladies numbered among its members such influential men as the Dukes of Beauvilliers and Chevreuse, and which also maintained close contact with the mystical life of well-disposed Protestants, pietists, and Quakers from England, Germany and the Netherlands. In contrast to the non-confessional Madame Guyon, Fénelon's dream was to make the Catholic Church the haven of

[11] J. M. B. de la Motte-Guyon, *Règle des associés à l'enfance de Jésus* (Lyons, 1685), p. 87.

European enthusiasm, and to effect a reconciliation between mystical subjectivity and institutional ecclesial structures, thus at the same time effecting the fundamental reconciliation between a mystically more profound religiosity and a morality of reason valid in essence for all people. Fénelon, the friend of mystics, was also to his contemporaries a rather disturbing Ultramontane as well as the virtuous champion of the "natural religion", on the grave of which phenomenon D'Alembert's tears were to fall.

IV. The Mystery of the Self from the Viewpoint of Subjectivity and Objectivity

In the return to the stark light of every day, in the rejection of any "extraordinary light", lies the completion of Eckhart's and Tauler's self-abnegation. Instead, we have the "common way". Religious subjectivity renounces its particularity and in doing so also rejects the deepest impulse of the Enlightenment, namely the will to self-determination. The Enlightenment's involvement with mysticism was not actively pursued but came from "indifference". Mysticism is at once the realization and conquest of enlightenment, and it is conquest in so far as it rejects the will to power, which the Enlightenment, through the rule of nature, turned into an ideology. The self towards which the mystic retires from the sphere of objectivity proceeds from the indifferent to the *resignatio in infernum*. It was characteristic of Spanish mysticism and of St Francis de Sales that the empirical subject be surrendered to the sphere of objectivity. John of the Cross describes a situation in which the self finds itself given over to a total confusion of the sensual as of the intellectual faculties of the soul. All of them are experienced as real things. Thus we find among the mystics the beginnings of empirical psychology. Only the soul's foundation, its substance, enters into imageless union with the Godhead. Bossuet, the orthodox critic, called that quite simply "an exaggeration of a type common among mystics". Fénelon then interpreted this doctrine of the soul's foundation, the spark, *apex mentis*, or the summit of the soul, psychologically by stating that it is a matter of those acts that on account of their pure spontaneity and their freedom from all previous reference to the self-interest of the subject remain hidden from it. The mystery of the self, he said, was not the sort of puzzle that could be resolved by reflection alone. "*The riddle* does not exist." Anything that can be resolved by reflection is not the self. It belongs to homogeneous objectivity. Reflection therefore leads to confusion, from which emanates the total transcendence of pure love. The mystery of the self is this pure transcendence.

At this point I should like to advert once again to Wittgenstein. An entry in his journal runs: "It is the ego that is profoundly mysterious."[12] But another entry from the same period says: "This is the path that I have followed: idealism posits man as something unique in the world; solipsism sets me apart; and finally I observe that I too am a part of the rest of the world. Thus can conscientiously analysed idealism lead to realism."[13]

And in the *Tractatus* we read: "The self of solipsism shrinks to a point without extension, and there remains the reality coordinated with it" (5.64). This corresponds to the course of mystical experience. Does such experience add something to homogeneous, objectivized reality? It adds to it the consciousness that facts do not resolve the issue, that they "all contribute only to setting the problem, not to its solution" (6.4321).

But hasn't this already been noted by every other transcendental philosophy and do we have to call the concept of a transcendental subjectivity a mystical concept? Because we do not have to do so the content of transcendental philosophy remains permanently ambiguous and its possibility problematical. It is not in itself a persuasive way of thinking. It circumvents actuality while yet being bound by facticity. The transcendental self that becomes such in reflection is ambiguous. It experiences itself as outside time and above psychology. But at the same time it is only one particular instant in an individual historical process of reflection. It is not immune from psychological interpretation. In his *Sein und Zeit*, Heidegger reflected in transcendental terms on the facticity of existence and sought to think of death as a constitutive moment of this existence. But the philosophy of *Sein und Zeit* is also ambivalent. It diversified into existentialism, an anthropological philosophy that regarded

[12] *Schriften*, I, p. 173.   [13] *Schriften*, I, p. 178.

death as nonsense, as the refutation of all meaning and of transcendence, and into a way of thinking about being at the end of
which stood the extinction of subjectivity and the mystical conclusion of "composure".

But if we are to communicate the subject-object relationship,
the relationship between transcendence and facticity, then, as
Hegel observed in the Introduction to his *Phenomenology of
Mind*, we must always presuppose the immediate presence of
the absolute. Without such presence the dialectic would be none
other than what the positivists say it is. This is also true of the
negative dialectic of the Frankfurt School which, recalling the
Old Testament's condemnation of images, hopes to avoid pro-
faning truth by not naming it. In fact, behind this dialectic we
can discern not Hegel but Schopenhauer!

V. The Ambivalent Experience of the Absence of God. Immediacy versus Meaninglessness

Christian theology is obliged to name the absolute, and therein
lies its present embarrassment. For theology participates in the
process of enlightenment, the homogenization of experience
through science. Through modern exegesis its biblical sources
have become as much the targets of philosophical and historical
objectivization as any other texts. Where is it to obtain its
hermeneutical pre-understanding of the meaning of the Word
of God if this can no longer be presupposed as pragmatically
understood in a religious tradition beyond all question?

It has tried to do it in terms of transcendental philosophy. But
the attempt remains imprisoned by the ambiguity of such an
approach, which anyway has for long now been an anthropological one. We now have an anthropological theology and more
recently, as a result, a political theology and an historical-philo-
sophical theology, a theology in which the Word of God is
always a code for facts predominantly thought of as future. This
theology has almost nothing to say about death as a matter for
the individual but all the more about the death and absence of
God. But what meaning do these words have if even the word
God no longer has meaning? The meaninglessness of the
word God is a part of the teaching content of neo-positivist philos-

ophy. There we see very clearly the fact that all functional statements of the concept of God—God as guarantor of the moral
order, of political stability, of spiritual hygiene, and so on—have
had to give way before progressive enlightenment. But with that
it seems that even the principle of Occam's razor must be sacri-
ficed. It is no longer applicable.

But mysticism anticipated even that experience. Dom Chapman, a twentieth-century teacher of the mystical life influenced
by Caussade, writing of mystical prayer, says: "It is a condition
similar to idiocy and appears to be a total waste of time until
contemplation gradually becomes more lively. One can therefore
make the strange experience of suddenly asking oneself what the
point of it all is, whether one is not perhaps addressing someone
with mechanical formulas that say nothing. In such circumstances, the word 'God' does then seem to mean nothing. In
surrendering ourselves to this strange and richly contradictory
situation we are putting ourselves on the right road and must
beware of wanting to think about where God is, what he has
done for us, what we are to him, and so on. For such thoughts
take us out of our prayer and spoil God's dwelling in us, as
St John of the Cross said. St Anthony probably had the same
thing in mind when he said: 'No one prays properly if he still
knows who God is and what he is himself.' "[14]

The great mystics, particularly those of more recent history,
saw God's absence as the manner of his immediate presence.
Jesus' last words, "My God, my God, why hast thou forsaken
me?" were to them the perfect model of all mystical experience.
And, vice versa, only from this experience can we derive a non-
mythological understanding of what could be meant by sonship
of God. It is hard to see how theology will escape the alternatives of either becoming positive science or reverting to the
heteronomy of a largely fundamentalist approach to revelation,
if it fails to make use of the dimension of experience opened up
to us through mysticism.

But is it not possible that if applied to the present situation the
self-abnegation of mysticism could lead to total conformity?
What in its result distinguishes the mystical experience of God

[14] J. Chapman, *Spiritual Letters*.

as the total negation of all religious concepts from the banal reduction of man to his biological and need-dependent nature?
What characterizes wordless prayer from that madness, that, as
Chapman says, looks like idiocy? A parable might clarify the
question: a painter reduces a purely figurative painting through
a series of increasingly abstract concepts until he reaches the point
at which he is once again standing in front of a white canvas. Is
the last state of the canvas any different from the first? Not to
the observer, who sees only the result. But for the painter,
definitely—provided he bears in mind the process through which
it all happened. Similarly, if mystical immediacy is not to become
merely a return to nature it must not lose sight of its formative
development, the process that gave rise to it. In this respect it is
a little ingenuous of Wittgenstein to say, as he does in the conclud-
ing proposition of his *Tractatus*, that "anyone who understands
me eventually recognizes them [the propositions]as nonsensical"
when he has "climbed up beyond them" and thrown "away the
ladder" (6.54). This would be to ignore the nature of thought as
memory, as though in this case there was an "up there" that was
distinguished from down here by something other than the ladder
that led up to it. The Church has been right to mistrust the
quietist thought of a *moyen court* to mystical union. This also
sheds positive light on that peculiarity of Christian mysticism
which mystics of other convictions so often saw as concession and
irrelevance: the commemorative adherence to the biblical, religious and ecclesiastical way. Unless this way was ever kept in
mind and made present the goal relapsed back into its beginnings and the "dark night" of the mystic became instead a night
of confusion in which one thing could not be distinguished from
another. But by remaining mystically distanced while at the
same time never losing touch with the process that formed it,
religion could endure in a world that is the child of the scientific
enlightenment without becoming encapsulated by it and without
having to define itself in that world's categories.

Translated by Simon King

Johann Baptist Metz

A Short Apology of Narrative

CONTEMPORARY theological dictionaries are in some ways unreliable because they leave out so much—for example, the word "story" or "narrative". Harald Weinrich has shown in his contribution to this number what a serious gap in theological understanding is revealed by this absence. I should like, in this article, to write a short apology of narrative, especially since the category of "dangerous memory", which I used in a previous article in *Concilium*[1] to throw light on the understanding of Christian faith in our present situation clearly has a narrative structure.[2]

I cannot hope to deal systematically or fully here with the theological theme of narrative, but can only mention a number of different and significant points.[3] I have not attempted a linguistic analysis, partly because I am simply not competent to do so. Another reason is because it is not theologically relevant to incorporate the narrative potential of Christianity into a linguistic theory (in order to close it as a form of pre-scientific communication). An even more important reason is that narrative processes have to be protected, interrupted in order to justify them critically and even guided in the direction of a competent narra-

---

[1] "The Future in the Memory of Suffering", *Concilium*, June 1972 (American Edn., Vol. 76).
[2] I have discussed this in greater detail in my article "Erinnerung" in H. Krings, H. M. Baumgartner and C. Wild, eds., *Handbuch Philosophischer Grundebegriffe*, I (Munich, 1973).
[3] I have dealt with the significance of a memorative and narrative soteriology for the central theme of the history of redemption and freedom in "Erlösung und Emanzipation", *Stimmen der Zeit*, 98 (1973).

tive without allowing the experience of faith to be silenced like every original experience.

I. NARRATIVE AND EXPERIENCE

"However familiar we may be with the name, the narrator is not present for us, alive and active. Not only is he remote from us—he is always becoming more remote. It is as though an apparently inalienable and assured ability had been taken away from us. This is the ability to exchange experiences."[4] The atrophy of narrative is particularly dangerous in theology. If the category of narrative is lost or outlawed by theology as pre-critical, then real or original experiences of faith may come to lack objectivity and become silenced and all linguistic expressions of faith may therefore be seen as categorical objectivizations or as changing symbols of what cannot be said. In this way, the experience of faith will become vague and its content will be preserved only in ritual and dogmatic language, without the narrative form showing any power to exchange experience.

Theology is above all concerned with direct experiences expressed in narrative language. This is clear throughout Scripture, from the beginning, the story of creation, to the end, where a vision of the new heaven and the new earth is revealed. All this is disclosed in narrative. The world created from nothing, man made from the dust, the new kingdom proclaimed by Jesus, himself the new man, resurrection as a passage through death to life, the end as a new beginning, the life of future glory—all these show that reasoning is not the original form of theological expression, which is above all that of narrative. The logos of theology, so long as it conceals its own narrative form, is as embarrassed by them as reason is by questions concerning the beginning and the end and the destiny of what is new and has never yet been. The question about the beginning, the *archē*, which enabled the Greeks with their logos to break the spell of pure narrative in myth, leads thought straight back to narrative. The beginning and the end can only be discussed in narrative form— Kant was aware of this when he spoke of the "rhapsodic beginning of thought" which was not open to argumentative recon-

[4] W. Benjamin, "Der Erzähler", *Illuminationen* (Frankfurt, 1961), p. 409.

struction. Above all, what is new and has never yet been can only be introduced in narrative. As Adorno has observed in the closing passages of his *Minima Moralia*, if reason is closed to the narrative exchange of experiences of what is new and completely breaks off that exchange for the sake of its own critical nature and its autonomy, it will inevitably exhaust itself in reconstructions and become no more than a technique. This question will be discussed more fully in Sections IV and V below.

II. THE PRACTICAL AND PERFORMATIVE ASPECT OF NARRATIVE

There are examples of narrative traditions which resist the influence of our supposedly post-narrative age—for instance, the Hassidic stories, Johann Peter Hebel's or Bertolt Brecht's "calendar" stories or the "traces" of Ernst Bloch, whose main work, *Das Prinzip Hoffnung*, reads like a great encyclopedia of "hope" stories. They all illustrate the practical character of such narratives, their communication of an experience and close involvement of the narrator and the listener in the experience narrated. "Most born story-tellers pursue a practical interest. . . . This is indicative of the distinctive nature of all true stories, all of which have an overt or hidden use—a moral, a practical instruction, a rule of life. In every case, the story-teller is a man who knows what to do with the listener. . . . His stories are based on experience, either his own or other people's, which he transforms into the experience of those who listen to his stories."[5]

Martin Buber has reaffirmed this characteristic in his introduction to the Hassidic stories and has also drawn attention to other important features of the narrative form: "The story is itself an event and has the quality of a sacred action. . . . It is more than a reflection—the sacred essence to which it bears witness continues to live in it. The wonder that is narrated becomes powerful once more. . . . A rabbi, whose grandfather had been a pupil of Baal Shem Tov, was once asked to tell a story. 'A story ought to be told,' he said, 'so that it is itself a help,' and his story was this. 'My grandfather was paralysed. Once he was asked to tell a story about his teacher and he told how the holy Baal Shem Tov used to jump and dance when he was praying. My grandfather stood

[5] W. Benjamin, *op. cit.*, pp. 412 ff.

up while he was telling the story and the story carried him away so much that he had to jump and dance to show how the master had done it. From that moment, he was healed. This is how stories ought to be told.' "[6]

This text is remarkable for two reasons. In the first place, it is a successful example in a critical, post-narrative age of how narrative teaching can be linked with narrative self-enlightenment about the very interest which underlies the narrative process. In this case, the story is not ideologically unconscious of the interest that governs it. It presents this interest and "tries it out" in the narrative process. It verifies or falsifies itself and does not simply leave this to discussion about the story which lies outside the narrative process. This is, in my opinion, a very important aspect of the narrative form which cannot, unfortunately, be pursued further here.

In the second place, Buber's text points to an inner relationship between story and sacrament, in other words, to the story as an effective sign and to the narrative aspect of the sacrament as a sign. The sacramental sign can easily be characterized as a "linguistic action" in which the unity of the story as an effective word and as practical effect is expressed in the same process. The aspect of ceremony and ritual may perhaps mean that the sacrament is not clearly recognized as a saving narrative. On closer inspection, however, it is evident firstly that the linguistic formulae used in the administration of the sacraments are typical examples of what are known as "performative" expressions,[7] and secondly that they narrate something. The story form occurs, for instance, in the eucharistic prayer ("on the night that he was betrayed . . .") and the formula of the sacrament of penance is incorporated within the framework of a narrative action.

I am convinced that it is very important to bring out this narrative aspect of the sacrament more clearly. If this is done, the relationship between word and sacrament may be more fully elaborated theologically. Above all, it should also be possible to relate the sacramental action more closely to stories of life and suffering and to reveal it as a saving narrative.

[6] M. Buber, Werke III (Munich, 1963), p. 71.
[7] See J. L. Austin, How to do Things with Words (Cambridge, Mass., 1962).

III. The Pastoral and Social Aspect of Narrative

Marginal groups and religious sects are always active in society and it would be wrong for the churches *a priori* to silence or reject their disturbing message. Although the underlying ambiguity of the Jesus People, for example, prevents us from accepting them uncritically as providing the best chance of Christian renewal, they have one very positive merit—they and others employ, not argument and reasoning, but narrative. They tell the story of their conversion and retell biblical stories, sometimes in a patently helpless way that is open to manipulation. Is this simply a sign of spiritual regression, of the danger of archaism or infantilism in the religious life, of emotional, pseudo-religious enthusiasm or of an arbitrary and contemptuous rejection of serious theological reasoning? Or is it rather the visible appearance of something that is usually repressed in the public and official life of the churches? Are these marginal groups not in fact drawing on something that has for too long been hidden and neglected in Christianity, its narrative potential? Are they not remembering that Christians do not primarily form an argumentative and reasoning community, but a story-telling community and that the exchange of experiences of faith, like that of any "new" experience, takes a narrative form? Finally, does this not apply above all to the marginal groups which, in their refusal to speak the language of ritual and theology, are almost silent?

This is important in the question of pastoral care and the proclamation of faith, which are, I believe, in a critical situation because we are no longer able to narrate with a practical and socially critical effect and with a dangerous and liberating intention. For too long, we have tried to suppress the narrative potential of Christianity and have confined it to credulous children and old people, although it is these who are especially sensitive to false or substitute stories or to an illusory exchange of experiences. This is why, in giving renewed emphasis to narrative, it is important to avoid the possible misunderstanding that "story-telling" preachers and teachers will be justified in their narration of anecdotes, when what is required are arguments and reasoning. After all, there is a time for story-telling and a time for argument. There is a difference between the two which has to be recognized.

A second misunderstanding has also to be avoided, that of believing that to stress the narrative element in pastoral care, preaching and teaching is to withdraw into the purely private sphere or the aesthetic sphere of good taste. If they give this impression, our stories will only reveal the extent to which we have forgotten how to tell them. It is true that there are many different kinds of narrative—stories which pacify, those which relieve feelings, like political jokes made under a dictatorship, and those which conceal a quest for freedom and stir the listener to imitation. Stories are told by very wise men who have, as Heinrich von Kleist observed, "eaten a second time of the tree of knowledge" and by little people who are oppressed or have not yet come of age. These, however, tell not only stories which tempt them to celebrate their immature dependence or their oppressed state, but also stories which are dangerous and which seek freedom. Freedom and enlightenment, the transition from dependence to coming of age, are not achieved simply by giving up narrative language in favour of the art of reasoning possessed by those who are enlightened and those who claim it as their privilege. (The old problem of the relationship between intellectuals and the working classes has, I believe, its origins primarily in a misunderstanding among intellectuals of the emancipatory character of narrative language, just as the value of the narrative form which is at the basis of Christianity is so often underestimated by theologians.)

There can, of course, be no *a priori* proof of the critical and liberating effect of such stories, which have to be encountered, listened to and told again. But surely there are, in our post-narrative age, story-tellers who can demonstrate what "stories" might be today—not just artificial, private constructions, but narratives with a stimulating effect and aiming at social criticism, "dangerous" stories in other words. Can we perhaps retell the Jesus stories nowadays in this way?

IV. THE THEOLOGICAL ASPECT OF NARRATIVE—NARRATIVE AS THE MEDIUM OF SALVATION AND HISTORY

The emphasis given in the preceding section to the pastoral aspect of the story form might give the impression that narrative is above all useful in teaching and catechesis as an indispensable aid to applied theology, but that it does not affect the structure of theology itself in any way. This is, of course, not the intention at all—to say that the narrative form characterizes the proclamation of faith and rational argument theology is too superficial a distinction, suppressing the underlying structure of theology itself. In this section, then, the theological aspect of narrative and the inseparable connection between narrative and argument (explanation, analysis, and so on) will be discussed. In Section V, the categories used in this section, including that of a narrative history of suffering, will be discussed in greater detail.

The question as to how history and salvation can be related without each being diminished may be regarded as of central importance in contemporary theology. History is the experience of reality in conflict and contradiction, whereas salvation is, theologically speaking, their reconciliation by the act of God in Jesus Christ. An integral part of history is the suffering experience of non-identity through violence and oppression, injustice and inequality, guilt, finiteness and death. In this sense, history is always a history of suffering. (When all men enjoy, as they do now, equal opportunities in a classless society, it should not be difficult to regard history as a history of suffering, since it is precisely in such a period that man's self-destructive nihilism, his despair and boredom—what Ernst Bloch has called the "melancholy of fulfilment"—often becomes so apparent.)

Can the theology of salvation and of man's redemption and reconciliation through Jesus Christ really hold its own against this history of suffering and the non-identity of history? Does it not *a priori* avoid the suffering of historical non-identity and lead an unhistorical and therefore mythological existence above the heads of men who are humiliated and even destroyed by the burden of their own history of suffering? Does the accumulated suffering of history not result in theology becoming cynical towards history? Is there perhaps a theological mediation between salvation and history which has only been taken seriously as a history of suffering? Can this theological mediation exist without becoming reconciled in too ambitious and ultimately too speculative and too self-deceiving a way with this history of suffering or without salvation-history being suspended in view of this history of suffering? With variants, this is the central question of systematic theology today and I believe that purely rational theological arguments cannot provide an answer to it. I should like at this point to clarify this statement by referring to the solutions to this problem which have been suggested by modern theology.[8]

The first of these solutions can be described as the existential and transcendental interpretation of the relationship between salvation and history. The question here is whether salvation and history are not reconciled by an existential or transcendental reduction of history to "historicity" and by a withdrawal from the non-identity of history to a mysterious identity of existence or of the subject which cannot be expressed.

A second solution suggests that salvation is conditioned by the history of suffering, projected into the future and, out of respect for the non-identity of history as a history of suffering, kept so to speak at stake. One question which arises again and again in connection with this solution, however, is whether a salvation which is always at stake is in any way different from a saving utopia, of which only heuristic use can be made in the history of human freedom.

A third solution has been received with interest in the German-speaking countries especially and merits rather more detailed discussion. A connection between the history of salvation and that of suffering is to be found in referring this question back to the central question of the specifically Christian understanding of God, in other words, by reference to the theme of the Trinity. The non-identity of the history of suffering can therefore, with God's *kenosis* in Jesus' crucifixion in mind, be included in the trinitarian history of God, so that, as Moltmann has observed, suffering becomes "suffering between God and God".

This solution has been suggested by certain Protestant theologians following Karl Barth, especially E. Jüngel and J. Moltmann in his book on the crucified God and by Catholics following Karl Rahner's proposals regarding the unity of the immanent Trinity. Among the latter, H. Küng has touched on this question of the historicity of God in his interpretation of Hegel's christology and H. Urs von Balthasar has dealt with it penetrat-

[8] I have considered the relationship between salvation and history in some detail in the medium of man's history of suffering in my article mentioned in note 3 above.

ingly in his interpretation of the paschal mystery within the sphere of God's *kenosis* history understood in the trinitarian sense.

In view of these attempts to solve the problem, I should like to express a fundamental consideration here. The non-identity of the history of suffering cannot be cancelled out in a dialectical process of the trinitarian history of salvation in such a way that it preserves its historical character. This is because this non-identity is not the same as the negativity of the dialectical process. In any attempt to interpret the division in the history of man's suffering within this dialectical process, an exchange will take place between the negativity of suffering and the negativity of the dialectical concept of suffering. A purely conceptual reconciliation between the history of salvation as the expression of the history of the redemption accomplished in Jesus Christ and the history of man's suffering is, in my opinion, not possible, because it can only lead either to a dualistic gnostic perpetuation of suffering in God or to a reduction of suffering to the level of a concept. This dilemma cannot be resolved by any more subtle speculative reasoning. It can only be resolved if salvation and redemption in the non-identity of the history of suffering are approached in a different way.

This brings me to the formulation of the following thesis. A theology of salvation which neither conditions nor suspends the history of salvation nor ignores the non-identity of the history of suffering cannot be purely argumentative. It must also be narrative. It is fundamentally a memorative and narrative theology. A narrative memory of salvation would in no sense lead to a regressive confusion of the distinction that dominates our problem. On the contrary, it would enable salvation in history, which is, of course, a history of suffering, to be expressed without either salvation or history being diminished. The category of narrative memory both prevents salvation and redemption from becoming paradoxically unhistorical and subordinates them to the logical identity of dialectical mediation.

Narrative is unpretentious in its effect. It does not have, even from God, the dialectical key which will open every door and throw light on the dark passages of history before they have been trodden. It is not, however, without light itself. Pascal drew attention to this light in distinguishing, in his *Memorial*, between the narrated "God of Abraham, Isaac and Jacob" and the God of rational argument, the "God of the philosophers".

This narrative memory of salvation is above all not a purely *ad hoc* construction designed to solve our problem. It goes much deeper than this, making present the mediation of the history both of salvation and of man's suffering as encountered in the testaments of our faith. If this narrative memory is reduced by theology to a preliminary mythological stage in the Christian logos, then theology is clearly functioning uncritically with regard to the possibilities and the limits of expressing the Christian message positively in the experience of the non-identity of history.

It is often forgotten, in the theological criticism of mythology, that the narration of critical argument is inherent in theology as a mediating aspect of its content. This also has to be borne in mind in connection with historical criticism in theology. Without anticipating the content of the following section too much, it is important to point out here that there is a difference between regarding the historical question and the historical truth that is related to it as a problem that has been forced on Christianity in modern times and is therefore in this sense inevitable and as a medium in which the truth of Christianity and its saving message are originally expressed and identified. A purely argumentative theology which conceals its origin and does not make this present again and again in narrative memory inevitably leads, in the history of human suffering, to those many modifications in reasoning which result in the extinction of the identifiable content of Christian salvation. I do not intend this to be regarded as a reason for excluding argument from theology. There is no question of regressively obscuring the distinction between narrative memory and theological argument. It is much more a question of acknowledging the relative value of rational argument, the primary function of which is to protect the narrative memory of salvation in a scientific world, to allow it to be at stake and to prepare the way for a renewal of this narrative, without which the experience of salvation is silenced.

V. THE NARRATIVE STRUCTURE OF CRITICAL REASON

Does what I have suggested so far in this article not amount ultimately to an uncritical blurring of differences in view of the modern emphasis on critical reason? Is the idea of a history of human suffering not made arbitrary and unsuitable by modern historical criticism? How can narrative and criticism be reconciled with each other?

As a result of the triumph of historicism, all tradition, including the narrative and memorative tradition of Christianity, has been transformed into history, that is, into the object of a critical reconstruction of historical reason. As G. Krüger pointed out, the relationship between historical criticism and the past "not only presupposes that this past is past, but also clearly aims to strengthen and affirm this absence of present reality in what was in the past. History has taken the place of tradition and this means that it occupies that place."[9] Since this was written, a criticism of this historical reasoning has been developed, which does not accept without question the absence of memory and of tradition in the scientific world of today, the absence which has resulted from our preoccupation with historicism. This criticism has above all been developed in the context of modern hermeneutics and also of a practical and critical philosophy of history and society which is especially indebted to the practical philosophy of Kant and his successors and to the modern criticism of ideology, including the neo-Marxist and the psychoanalytical varieties of this.[10]

This criticism, which is based on the distinction between Moltmann's "knowledge and interest", is concerned with the fundamental themes of historical reason, with the "criticism of criticism" and with the need to expose the abstract will to criticism as an ideology which unquestioningly gives way to a supposed progress in the critical consciousness. This "criticism of criticism" is not a purely formal meta-criticism which transposes the problem on to a purely theoretical plane. It deals rather with the problem as one of practical reason which occurs within certain historical memorative and narrative traditions. In this sense, history is—not as reconstructed history, but as memorative and narrative traditions—immanent in reason, which, in this criticism,

[9] G. Krüger, "Die Bedeutung der Tradition für die philosophische Forschung", *Studium Generale*, 4 (1951), pp. 322 ff.
[10] A detailed discussion of the whole question outlined in this section will be found in my article "Erinnerung", *op. cit.*, note 2.

becomes practical reason. The theme of narrative memory inevitably occurs again and again in this context and, what is more, it is in this case critical with regard to historical reason, which itself becomes more and more a technology looking back at the past and finally a "history" processed into a data bank, a computer memory without narrative and unable either to remember or to forget.

As Theodor Adorno observed, "Forgetting is inhuman because man's accumulated suffering is forgotten—the historical trace of things, words, colours and sounds is always the trace of past suffering. This is why tradition is nowadays confronted with an insoluble contradiction. It is not present and cannot be evoked, but as soon as all tradition is extinguished, inhumanity begins."[11]

Anyone who does not accept this almost insoluble difficulty will inevitably insist that there must be renewed respect for the history of man's suffering in our critical consciousness. This intention will only strike critical reason as obsolete if this respect for the history of suffering is denied because of a fear of heteronomy and if the authority of those who suffer is consequently destroyed in the interest of an abstract autonomy of reason. Whenever this respect is, however, preserved, then reason becomes in a sense "perceptive" in a way that cannot be expressed in the usual contrast which is made between authority and knowledge and which forms the most common framework for any discussion of the problem of the autonomy of reason. In this perception, history, as a remembered history of suffering, acquires for reason the form of a "dangerous tradition", which is passed on not in a purely argumentative manner, but as narrative, that is, in "dangerous stories".

These dangerous stories break through the spell of a historical reconstruction based on abstract reason and repudiate any attempt to reconstruct man's consciousness from the abstract unity of "I think". Above all, they show that man's consciousness is a consciousness which is "entwined in stories", which always has to rely on narrative identification and which, when the relative importance of the magisterium of history has been recognized, cannot entirely do without the magisterium of stories. In his film

[11] T. W. Adorno, "Thesen über Tradition", *Ohne Leitbild* (Frankfurt, 1967), pp. 34 ff.

Fahrenheit 451, François Truffault presented in a most vivid form this "consciousness in stories", which is nourished by the accumulated narrative potential that is derived from books, as a refuge of resistance, the only alternative to a world of total manipulation and absence of freedom.

VI. SOME QUESTIONS IN CONCLUSION

I should like to conclude by asking a number of questions that arise in connection with this short apology of narrative. How, for example, can the term narrative or story be defined more precisely? It cannot, after all, be regarded as synonymous with the term "historical account", since non-historical forms of knowledge or communication, such as the saga, fairy-tale or legend, have a narrative structure. What is the relationship between fiction and authenticity in narrative texts? What does it mean when we say that a story is "true" and in what sense can we speak of a narrative disclosure of truth? What relationship is there between narrated time and physical time? How are the story and the story-teller related to each other and how does the difference between the story and the story-teller prevent us from regarding narration as a pure textual problem?

In connection with the undoubted presence of narrative aspects in the individual sciences, we are bound to ask whether these are of merely secondary importance and of purely heuristic value. Have change, continuity and discontinuity in the sciences and in examples of narrative form to be made explicit in logic? Does our insistence on the narrative structure of theology not give rise to renewed questions about the scientific nature of theology and the cognitive character and the binding force of theological propositions?

Finally, among other questions, there is that of the historical Jesus—how are the history of Jesus and the stories of Jesus related? Has the canon of the Old and New Testaments not caused a "ban" to be imposed on narrative, preventing a retelling or further telling of stories in accordance with the contemporary situation? And should the meaning of the distinction between canonical and apocryphal stories not be re-examined?

Translated by David Smith

PART II
BULLETIN

Jean Mansir

The Fate of Two "Catechisms" in France

THE title of this article is rather cryptic, but under its heading I shall attempt to answer the question put to me by the editors of this number—how successful have the recently translated *"Dutch Catechism"* and *"Isolotto Catechism"*[1] been in their attempt to give new life and meaning to religious language in France? Before all else, I must warn the reader that this article is based not on copious and extensive research but simply on the opinions of various individuals and on the general impressions gained from the author's contact with a number of Christian groups in France. There is still room for a more systematic sociological study. Nevertheless, I hope that what follows will be of some interest to the reader.

I. THE BASIC QUESTION

In attempting to evaluate these two catechisms in their attempt to bring religious language alive, I shall firstly consider their content and then make some observations on the use of the two books in the actual process of catechesis. Both approaches of course will be concerned in some way with the problem of "language", although in rather different ways. The first will be con-

---

[1] *Une introduction à la foi catholique, le nouveau catéchisme*, published in France under the direction of Charles Ehlinger (Paris, 1968); published in English as *A New Catechism with Supplement* (London and New York, 1970); J. Servien, *L'Expérience chrétienne de l'Isolotto*, followed by *A la rencontre de Jésus* (Paris, 1969).

cerned with the language in which the two books are presented and the second with language in the general sense, as a means of establishing human contact and communication.[2] Naturally, the second of these two will prove more interesting and indeed I believe that it is this line of research that is going to have important and revolutionary effects upon the development of catechesis in the post-Conciliar Church.[3]

Although it is difficult to gain a general impression of the work that is being done in this area and even more difficult to make an analysis of it, we should not underestimate the role and importance of printed catechisms in the growth of our understanding of "language". But why, one might well ask, make a study of these two catechisms in this context? Neither of them even originated in France. The answer is that they were intended to be used outside their country of origin and it is therefore interesting to study how successfully they have crossed national and social frontiers. More than this, they have both achieved some degree of notoriety by the controversy they have aroused in the Church as a whole. In many ways the publication of these two catechisms can be seen as a prelude to a renewal of the "language" of faith.

II. PUBLISHING HISTORY OF THE TWO CATECHISMS

1. The difference between the commercial success of the two catechisms is instructive, because their literary forms are very different. The Dutch Catechism was published as a manual for adults designed for easy reference and published in the hope that it would be widely adopted. Very few will have assessed the book before buying it and fewer still will have worked out what use could be made of the book in catechesis. It is, after all, very convenient to have a summary of the faith at one's disposal —a book which takes various theological themes and summarizes the different standpoints taken in the Church today. This point is

---

[2] Cf., for example, the distinction that Merleau-Ponty makes between the "spoken word" and the "speaking word" in his book, *Phenomenology of Perception* (New York and London, 1946).

[3] An article which is most instructive in this context is the one by J. Le Du, "Language Problems and Catechetics", *Concilium*, March 1970 (American Edn., vol. 53).

particularly relevant to this article, for the French publishers of the catechism have printed with the book a supplement which attempts to outline the principal points of disagreement between the Dutch editors and the Roman theological commission appointed by the Pope to assess the book. The Dutch Catechism has had a quite phenomenal success in France—the sales have been in the region of 100,000 copies,[4] a figure seldom achieved in the publishing of religious books and we can be assured that the book has enjoyed the very widest circulation. The Isolotto Catechism is very different, being composed of short sentences and lavishly illustrated, intended as it is for young children. The "catechism" forms the last third of a book which is designed to convey the experience of Isolotto as a whole, that is, to give an overall impression of one particular situation in the contemporary Church. In this way, it is also designed to give some insight into the concentrated research into the pastoral mission of the Church that has been going on at Isolotto itself. The book is rather exceptional and it may take more than a first reading to grasp the enormous potential it has for teaching the faith to young children. This fact must be borne in mind when one considers the book's sales. The publisher has not supplied exact figures but we can accept his statement that the sales have been very limited indeed up till now.

2. How far have these two books achieved the purpose for which they were written? This is rather more difficult to answer. It is perhaps surprising that I have yet to find in France a group of Christians who actually use either of the two catechisms as a basis for thinking out the implications of their faith. Nor have I found any group in France using either as a basis for catechesis and this conclusion is based on questioning a very wide range of people responsible for Christian education at national and diocesan level. Of course, I am not stating categorically that it is impossible to find groups of people in France who are using the catechisms for either of these purposes, simply that if there are any they must be very few in number. This fact must pose rather serious questions.

As to individual readers to whom I have spoken (and I am

[4] A figure supplied by the publisher in December 1972.

speaking here mainly of the Dutch Catechism) their reactions could be summarized as follows: while they have been unanimous in saying that there is much interesting material here, the content does not seem to them to relate very closely to the religious climate in which they were brought up. Moreover, there seems to be a lot of unfamiliar theological jargon which is part of the general criticism that the concerns of the material seem rather far removed from their needs. They admit that much of the language is attractive and that it "sounds good" but in the last analysis it does seem to be the product of an experience which does not really tally with that of ordinary people in the modern world. About the time of publication in France (1968) people were gripped by the Dutch Catechism because it was so obviously far removed from the language of the old Tridentine formulae, but in retrospect it seems clear that the novelty of the language did not really answer the basic need—it did not address itself to the real dilemmas posed by the life of faith.[5]

III. The Reasons for the Fate of the Catechisms

I shall attempt to sort out some of the reasons for the demise of these two catechisms, which do not seem to have had the effect or the influence which their commercial sales would suggest. I shall consider the books separately as the factors involved are very different in each case and are even rather contradictory.

1. *The Dutch Catechism*

Naturally it is to be hoped that the present tension between local Churches and the Holy See will be eased and equally that there will be some change in the rather intransigent attitude of Roman theologians. But it is not my belief that to transfer the power to issue directives from the Vatican to national episcopal conferences would solve any of the problems. The fundamental problem is the inadequacy of the language we use to express our faith. The rather special circumstances of the origin of the Dutch Catechism resulted in its theological standpoint being somewhat partisan. It originated in fact when the Dutch bishops decided

[5] See the article by Tjeu van den Berk, "Language in the Dutch Catechism", *Concilium*, March 1970 (American Edn., vol. 53).

"to serve the reader by showing him the Christian message as a connected whole" in a catechism which would make believers "one in heart and soul with the whole, wonderful Catholic Church in which men live together, in spite of differences of race, culture and mentality". The Dutch Catechism claims that "the whole message, the whole of the faith remains the same", but it explicitly attempts "to render faithfully the renewal which found expression in the Second Vatican Council".[6]

The result of this was as follows: the completed work had the official approval of the Dutch bishops and was, by its very nature, the product of the work of scholars. The emphasis was on presenting a summary of Catholic doctrine and underlining the continuity with tradition and the essential unity of the faith. But the point to be noted is that it begins with the received doctrine of the Church and then tries to meet the daily experience of people by diluting the eternal truths of the faith.[7]

Now it can well be argued that this was indeed justifiable for those who actually run the institutional Church and it may well be pointed out that this approach has the great virtue that it underlines the formal unity of the Church and of the faith. But at the same time my contention is that this renders impossible a general renewal of the language of faith. (This fact should be borne in mind when we come to examine the Isolotto Catechism.) But the fundamental truth to which this conclusion points is the very nebulous nature of a unity which is represented solely by doctrinal unity.

Outside France, many are often amazed that the French hierarchy have remained so silent in the current theological ferment. They suggest that the Church in France may be exhausted by the courage and audacity of its pre-conciliar movements towards reform. But to me the silence is attributable to something quite different: it is simply a question of the "declergification" of the Church, if I may be permitted to use such a word. French bishops and theologians have decided to listen to their people, to let the people themselves speak instead of handing out advice and pro-

---

[6] *A New Catechism, op. cit.*, pp. vii and v.
[7] Tjeu van den Berk, "Language in the Dutch Catechism", *op. cit.*, pp. 86 ff. My judgment here is severe, but I am in agreement with what van den Berk says about the "mythological language" of the catechism.

nouncements. In many places the people have thus learned that they have a vital role to play in renewing the language of faith, a renewal which takes place in the light of their own Christian experience. Of course these are only the first rumblings which are as yet inadequate and are not nearly capable of being gathered together for general consumption. It will take time; there will be difficulties and many mistakes but these will be an essential part of the process of "purifying" the faith. The majority of people who are concerned in this way to build up the articulation of their faith from the basis of their Christian experience find that the Dutch Catechism means little to them.

2. *The Isolotto Catechism*

It will have become clear by now that the factors we have been discussing are unlikely to have much bearing on the Isolotto Catechism. Called in Italian an "encounter with Jesus" (*Incontro a Gesù*) and subtitled *A Guide for Initiating the Young into the Mystery of Christ*, what it conveys above all is an *experience*. And this experience is the experience of a particular Christian community, the community of Isolotto. The origin of the work was in the needs of the men, women and children of that community in the context of their daily lives, lives with a human and a Christian dimension. A Christian grass-roots community, structured as a parish, in the traditional sense and fully integrated into the community as a whole of one of the poorest areas of Florence. The bias of this community was not derived from some theoretical unity of the faith but from concrete daily life, the *praxis* of the community itself and this with the object of understanding life at its deepest, in the light of Christian faith. So it was not for the community of Isolotto a question of "presenting the faith of our fathers in a form suitable to the present day" (Dutch Catechism, p. v), but on the contrary of understanding the reality of living the faith day by day. The object was not to go round catechizing people but rather that people and pastor should be involved together in a process of self-catechesis, if one may so put it. But children have to be initiated into the process and equally the virility of the language of faith depends on feed-back from the community itself.

It would be simple to criticize the Isolotto Catechism, but let us remember that in some sense the experience has emerged because the ecclesiastical authorities have in no way been concerned with it. The bishop had nothing to do with the research on which it is based though he has managed to ensure that what the community of Isolotto has done shall not be imitated elsewhere.

We will not dwell either upon the incompleteness of this "catechism" for it was certainly not this that caused its lack of popularity in France. It has a particularity about it and it is precisely this which makes it so interesting. Indeed I would suggest that it is this fact that points to the real source for a renewal of religious language. But this same particularity is obviously the reason for its lack of success outside Isolotto, and why in turn I would suggest why it is unlikely to become the model for a renewal of religious language in the Church as a whole. But it could be, it might be possible that it could serve in France as a model for all those groups who wish to begin the process by examining the reality of their own experience. But there will never be two Isolotto catechisms for there is only one Isolotto.

IV. CONCLUSION

By comparing the fate of these two catechisms in France, we have touched on the fundamental problems facing those concerned with a renewal of religious language. The genuine concern for the unity of faith could well paralyse the creative expression of our actual experience here and now. We all too cautiously hide behind the curtain of *aggiornamento*, forgetting or ignoring the basic unity between existence and language. We tend to pursue our abstract notion of unity and universality. We forget the praxis-orientated nature of faith. Any attempt at a genuine re-creation of the language of faith must emerge from the concrete situation. In this way only will we achieve a language that "speaks", and even then it will only speak to people who are involved in the situation from which it arises.

The problem of drawing out the implications of this for the Church as a whole seems insoluble. It is all too easy to envisage the risks of sectarian interest and the atomizing of the Church and its faith.

But the question may be insoluble because it is ill-conceived. So many confused issues are involved. But let us never identify the deposit of faith entrusted to the universal Church with expressions of faith which arise from the explorations of those whose aim is an "encounter with Jesus". The real act of catechesis is rather like the long journey of the people of Israel—from their origins among the pagan myths to the time when they recognized in Jesus the fulfilment of God's promise to mankind. Maybe every one of us, theologian, bishop or ordinary believer, will have his part to play in this long journey, though let us not forget that it is a journey undertaken in the context of the fullness of the revelation of God entrusted to the universal Church, like an inalienable treasure. The crisis of religious language compels us to some kind of silence but it also calls to dialogue and to the creating of a language which is living because it is lived.

Translated by Robin Baird-Smith

Jerry Gill

Religious Expression and the
Language of Popular Culture

IT IS time we rid ourselves of the delusion that we can understand
our own age. I seriously doubt that more than a handful of
people have ever understood their own epoch—and the rapidity
of change in our time may well have rendered this élite class
quite extinct. We seem to be confronted with three broad alternatives: either (1) Western civilization is in the process of decaying,
or (2) it is merely in a transitional stage of its continued growth,
or (3) we are on the brink of an altogether new level of human
existence. Although there is some merit in determining the implications of these alternatives for the Christian way of being
in the world, it is essential to recall that in the final analysis the
Christian way must have its own integrity. And so in seeking to
gain some insight into various forms of "secular" religious expression today, I shall minimize inferences concerning overall
cultural significance.

Rather than trace the development of religious expression in
specific movements and sub-cultures, I shall simply call attention
to the three main dimensions of contemporary English-speaking
popular culture which cut across many boundaries and within
which the expression of religious concerns seem highly, though
perhaps surprisingly, relevant. I shall focus on current slang,
popular music and radical political rhetoric. Throughout it is
important to bear in mind that in much of contemporary experience the line between linguistic and non-linguistic expression is
increasingly difficult to locate. The closest I can come to marshal-
ling a thesis is to contend that amidst all the various and bizarre

features of popular culture there are many which carry religious meaning.

I

It can be argued that slang provides a clue to the character and direction of a culture. One trend in current slang which can be singled out is the predominance of what might be called "somatic" symbolization. There is a tendency to employ terms and images which pertain to physical embodiment and tactile experience. "Dig" ("dig it", "dig this", "can you dig it?", etc.) and "groove" ("groovin", "groovey", etc.) are examples that come quickly to mind. The electric connotations of terms such as "vibrations" ("good vibes", etc.) and "turn on", as well as "tripping" and "mind blowing" also underscore the somatic or physical character of much of contemporary slang.

It may not be too far-fetched to suggest that this tendency to somatic symbolization is of a piece with other manifestations of rebellion against the dominance of Western culture by mentalistic, sequential thinking. From Plato and Aristotle through Descartes and Locke to Russell and Sartre, Western thought—on both the popular and the intellectual level—has focused on concepts which play up the role of the mind as the key to understanding and health. Today many people are reasserting the importance of the body, and this concern reveals itself in popular language as well as in the philosophies of Merleau-Ponty and the Skinnerian behaviourists.

Another form of slang which has become of major importance today is that of the simple hand gesture. In fact, it is quite surprising how many things one can say using only one hand. Think of Churchill's victory sign, thumbs up (and down), the pope's blessing, the sign for "O.K.", the peace sign, the bird, and the "power to the people" sign. The instant and universal "political" significance of these hand signals is truly amazing. They provide a sort of universal language that spans nearly all age groups, nationalities and languages.

Yet another, though non-linguistic, form of expression today is variety of clothing styles. Admittedly, much of the original thrust of this radical departure from the traditions of the last hundred years has been blunted by the capitalistic opportunism of designers and advertisers. Nevertheless, it is the case that people today seek to speak by means of their clothes far more than has ever been possible in previous times. Conformity still abounds, of course, but this does not negate the fact that clothing styles are a powerful means of expression in contemporary culture.

What of the religious significance of all these phenomena? The trend towards somatic symbolization, despite the dangers of over-simplification, seems to me to be of immense value from a Christian point of view. Far too long have we been tyrannized by dualistic theories and images which value the mind above the body. Such dualisms are out of harmony with the holistic perspective of the Bible in general and with the concepts of incarnation and bodily resurrection in particular. The popularity and power of hand signs would seem to indicate at once a desire for universal communication and a kind of revolutionary, secret-society tendency, not unlike New Testament times. The so-called "Jesus people" have even devised their own hand-sign; the index finger pointed towards heaven to indicate that Jesus is the one way to God. The variety of clothing styles can be seen as an insistence on people's right and need to be free from what Paul called "conformity to the world". While such an insistence is worthy of honour within the Christian ethic, freedom *from* old structures is not necessarily freedom *for* newness of life.

It is important to think and feel deeply about the significance of all these things for religion. It is far too easy to dismiss them out-of-hand as aberrations of a confused and/or evil society—or to adopt them forthwith as necessary new wine skins. By and large the Christian response has been strangely dichotomized along these lines. Perhaps the most pathetic posture is that which adopts the new forms of expression in only a surface fashion, without changing the basic features of its traditional position. Having folk-rock singing groups on the platform, being a "Jesus freak", and talking about "turning on with Christ" is as bad as the more recent tradition of having famous athletes give commercials for God, devising Madison Avenue techniques for explaining the gospel, and giving discount stamps for church attendance. All of these things have less integrity than *either* remaining strictly traditional *or* reducing the gospel entirely to humanism.

II

A perhaps more familiar form of expression with a bearing on religion is that of contemporary popular music. I am not in a position to speak knowingly about classical and electronic music, and romantic ballads and "Bubblegum Rock" will not bear much scrutiny. There are three forms of popular music, however, which are especially important for our overall theme; they are "hard rock", folk rock and soul.

Hard rock got its most powerful impetus from the Beatles, though it had earlier roots in America with the likes of Elvis Presley and Chuck Berry. Since the Beatles this emphasis has been carried on by many groups, most notably the Jefferson Airplane, Jimi Hendrix, and the Rolling Stones. Although the lyrics of hard rock are important in and of themselves, it is the driving rhythm, the novel acoustics and the volume of the medium which carry the clearest message. It has been suggested that hard rock represents the upsurge of Dionysian power, rebelling against the Apollonian order that has traditionally characterized Western civilization, especially in the modern, scientific era. The message of hard rock is that the old values and standards are too confining to the human spirit, too dependent upon mentalistic, artificial images of human existence. Moreover, it is a protest against the meaninglessness of the technological age, providing a way of escape and release through improvisation, lack of inhibition and sensory "overload". While there is no denying that this is a much needed emphasis in our time—and that it may well represent a quest for the authentic ecstasy which used to be provided by religion—it is perhaps an emphasis that leads to its own kind of imbalance.

Folk rock focuses much more attention on the lyrics than does hard rock, but its message is very much the same. It grew out of folk music and was firmly established as a genre by Bob Dylan—who is still very much alive. Others, such as Simon and Garfunkle, Leonard Cohen, Donovon and James Taylor, have made lasting contributions. In many ways, this form of music functions as the conscience of the young generation. Quite often the poetry is outstanding, and the message combines a very strong love and peace ethic with a deep awareness of the incongruities and mysteries of human existence. It is clear that there is a great deal of overlapping between the main themes of folk rock and the concerns of religion. It is to be hoped that such overlapping can produce much needed dialogue.

Soul music is, of course, an almost strictly American phenomenon. Nevertheless it has important significance from a religious point of view if only because it grew out of blues and jazz on the one hand and gospel music on the other. Gospel music had developed side by side with blues and jazz, but in the past decade the two types of music have to a large extent merged into soul. The blues expressed the black man's struggle as a slave, jazz represented his existence as a second-class citizen in industrial and war-time America, and soul gives expression to the Afro-American Renaissance of the 1960s. In addition to its obvious message concerning the naturalness of sexuality—something the white West knows very little about—soul music reflects a deep concern and marital loyalty and the existential difficulties of oppressed peoples.

The king of soul has always been James Brown. After the defection of such groups as The Supremes and The Temptations —both co-opted by the white media magnates—Brown's court has been filled with people such as Aretha Franklin, Wilson Pickett and Ike and Tina Turner. Several years ago Ray Charles said that the role of Jesus in gospel music had been taken over by the woman in soul music—salvation comes through a faithful woman. There is, to be sure, an understandable bias against religion among young blacks because it has for so long been used as a method of keeping them "in their place". It does not seem likely that much can be done in the near future by way of overcoming this unfortunate situation. What faith there is among young blacks is derived from and directed towards their own cause, which at least in some ways is as it should be. None the less, it can be argued that to a large degree the black person's courage and endurance are directly traceable to his deep religious involvement.

III

A third dimension of contemporary popular culture which carries important religious ramifications is radical political rhetoric. On the one hand there are the activists who seek a utopia beyond the revolution, and on the other hand there are the advocates of the counter-culture, also seeking a utopia after a revolution, but of a quite different sort. These two forms of political radicalism differ significantly in both aim and method. Whereas the activists—be they Marxists or some other brand— generally talk of an ideal society in which technology is put to humane use, the counter-culturists speak in terms of a "back to nature", communal society. In addition, the activists are convinced that the ideal society can only be ushered in by means of political revolution, necessarily involving a certain amount of violence. The counter-culturists, on the other hand, maintain that by keeping participation in the established culture to a minimum and simultaneously developing an alternative culture they will bring about the collapse of the former and the full bloom of the latter.

It should be immediately apparent that the concerns of radical politics are in many ways similar to the concerns of religion. Unfortunately, however, Western religion has long been associated with the values and institutions of established society. Thus the similarity of concerns gets blurred over, both for religionists and for political radicals. The similarities include such points as a common concern for the well-being of mankind, a common conviction that much if not most of modern society is bad for mankind, and a shared belief that nothing short of a total re-ordering of values will set the world aright. The last two points are explicitly denied by establishmentarian politicians and religionists alike. As Kierkegaard reminds us, it is difficult to be a Christian in Christendom! Not only do political and religious radicalism stand together against "status quoism", they are also opposed to the assumption of both secular and religious liberalism that the ideal society can and will be realized through progressive reform. To proceed along the present course is not to arrive at salvation.

There are, to be sure, important differences between the

rhetoric of political radicalism and that of Christianity. Perhaps the most important one is that whereas the former argues that things will inevitably get worse and then better, the latter argues that such political ups and downs are essentially irrelevant. In other words, political radicals maintain an apocalyptic stance which envisions the ideal society within history, while Christianity affirms that the ideal society will come from beyond history, not by the activity of men, but by the activity of God. The apocalypticism of radical activists is like that of the Zealots in New Testament times. That of counter-culturists is like that of the Essenes. In both cases the way of life is dependent on the realization of the ideal—the end justifies the means. The Christian way of life is dependent on its own integrity—it is an end in itself.

Finally, a word about the relationship between the foregoing reflections and the overall theme of this issue. The crisis in religious language extends to at least three broad fronts: the philosophical, the theological and the cultural. The first pertains to the semantic legitimacy of God-talk, the second to the problems of coherence and integrity within the religious community, and the third to the relationship between the religious community and the society in which it finds itself. Clearly, the concerns of the present essay lie almost exclusively in the latter category. Nevertheless, these three dimensions of the crisis are inextricably related and each needs to be considered in the light of the others. This issue of *Concilium* would seem to provide an excellent point of departure for such a full-orbed consideration.

Rogério de Almeida Cunha

Illiteracy and the Development of Self-Awareness in the Thought of Paulo Freire

I. Introduction

PAULO FREIRE, on the basis of his experience in the field of education, working both on his own and as a member of a team, has sketched out the various stages in what he calls "the development of self-awareness" ("conscientization") to be achieved through basic education. His aim is to make men face the facts of their existence. His activity and thought began from his efforts in the field of teaching adult illiterates, which made him well known and had a profound influence on the development of his ideas. But this basic education, he says, is merely a stage in the task of developing self-awareness, and cannot be separated from this wider endeavour. This development is a basic task, far wider than education in the strict sense, confers a humanizing character on education, and is what Freire called "political education".

Method as Educative Technique: The Phases

Paulo Freire invented or rediscovered a series of psycho-social and educational techniques, but the inner movement he gave them and the thought they presuppose and develop are more important than the techniques themselves. The sequence of events forces both educators and pupils to face up to the facts of their own existence (phases one and three—see below), so as to draw from these the elements best suited to develop an attitude of self-examination and communication (phases one and three).

Starting from the reality they live and the facts they observe, those taking part discuss these, meeting in "cultural circles", with the aim of finding a "new life". Verbal discussion then leads to the written exercise of finding new words. This leads in turn to thinking about creative activity and the freedom needed for creative thought (phases four and five). The essence of the method, as the development of self-awareness or as education, is therefore the approach of outgoing and free dialogue intimately linked to the verbal discussion.[1]

The following five phases can be distinguished:

1. Raising the level of vocabulary and thought patterns in the communities concerned. This is achieved by a group sharing the daily life of the communities and initiating informal discussions on their situation in the light of history.

2. Choice and arrangement of the words to be used to stimulate the educative process. These must be drawn from the vocabulary and thought patterns established in phase one, and be arranged in such a way that they gradually embrace all the phonetic phenomena of the language; but, most important of all, they must be charged with a meaningful content of relationship to history, present existence, emotions and challenge to the existing order.

3. Making out "codifications" of the themes and words generated. These take the form of faithful representations of scenes from or aspects of local life, using drawings, photographs, short films, transparencies, lectures or the like.

4. Establishing a card index system as an aid to co-ordinating discussions.

5. Making out "discovery" cards for use by the pupils. These contain the words generated, divided into syllables and into phonetic groups, so that they can be used in the "creation" of new words.

In all the phases it is essential to create and develop an attitude of respectful, loving and problem-seeking discussion, whether in the "investigation of themes", in the "discussions in cultural circles" or in the straightforward "educative sessions".

---

[1] The basic tool used in the development of self-awareness through education is the debate in "cultural circles". For this, see P. Freire, *Pedagogy of the Oppressed* (New York, 1972) and *idem, Educação como Prática da Liberdade* (Rio de Janeiro, 1967).

II. METHOD AS A SYSTEM OF THOUGHT

1. *The Basic Thesis: An Anthropological Concept of Culture*

The thought resulting from the application of such a method embraces the most varied aspects of human life. It has to be interdisciplinary and requires group discussion (phases one and three). The anthropological approach involved tends to be one that recognizes the dynamism and dialectical tension that exist between man and his everyday life (phases three and five), and that spring from a deliberate historical examination of this dialectical relationship. The basic "thesis" is that all men are capable of action, of expressing themselves, of communicating their thought—of creating culture, in fact. Culture, for Paulo Freire, is the sum of all that comes from men's hands as a result of conscious action. Man exercises his creative function, expresses himself and communicates through culture. In this way, he becomes ever more free—"he creates his freedom"; he becomes more social, he "forms a society", socializes himself. Culture is therefore, on the one hand, everything that man does consciously. On the other hand it is the product of all that is done, of the outcome of the dialectical tension between activity and thought. So, in its most humanizing sense, culture must necessarily include creativity, self-expression, communication, freedom and socialization.

2. *Illiteracy as an Historical and Political Problem*

"The very way a man looks at the world makes him a cultural being." Illiteracy does not mean a lack of culture, still less a lack of cultural capacity: it springs initially simply from lack of knowledge of a written code of expression. Now a written code of expression is normally used in the bosom of a society in order to produce a graphic synthesis of the verbal expression of the way men see their own reality, as well as of thought and communication. So some societies regard the illiterate as a "non-cultural" being, because they identify culture with the stage or type of cultural product that they have reached. Their socio-economic climate deprives men of the possibility of expressing themselves, of communicating creatively, even of perceiving, or indeed having, a reality of their own, except within the canons laid down by society.

These societies condition man in such a way that he is turned in on himself and creates a series of unreal explanations for human existence, and is thereby forced to continue under the sway of naïve or magical myths. These magical myths are evidence of man's irrepressible creativity and power of thought, but, being unreal, they are also indications of the alienation of those who are affected by them. Under these circumstances, being illiterate is the result of oppression brought about by the maintenance of socio-economic structures that feed the privileges of minorities whose interests are served by their own perpetuation.

The problem is therefore not so much one of illiteracy as one of oppression, and a genuine education will have to include and presuppose the development of self-awareness, that is, the exercise of thought about one's own situation, arising from a consciousness freed from myths and fatalism and exercising its own creativity in growing historical freedom, expressiveness and communicativeness. Otherwise, education is merely a mechanical process. The result is a process of integration in an open, historically dynamic society. Development of self-awareness both supposes and activates social and political liberation, and this is why the problem moves from the area of education, strictly so-called, into that of emancipation and liberation. "Education is shown to be an anthropology" and "tends to dictate a political approach".[2]

3. Dialectic, History and Socialization

The dynamism of Freire's system of thought and political and educational activity is therefore a dialectical tension which, in this case, means, at least initially, a dynamism that reciprocally opposes various poles, that tends to repeat itself on an increasing scale and to eliminate the negative approaches of those taking part in the discussion, and so eventually "negativism as such". Such a dialectical tension is the fruit of a conscious perception of the opposing points of view, of itself and of the negatives involved, which it tends to overcome. It derives from a capacity to

[2] Cf. M. Schooyans, "Une maieutique libératrice: la méthode de Paulo Freire", in Cultures et développement (Louvain, 1970), pp. 435-51; also, E. Fiori, "Learning to Speak their Word", Preface to Pedagogy of the Oppressed, op. cit.

stand back from oneself, to criticize, to criticize oneself and to surpass oneself. In the final analysis, it is the mark of the human dynamism of transcendence or self-transcendence. Surpassing or transcending oneself is then the consequence of a dialectical process between a real or actual consciousness—a "maximum possible" consciousness in the given circumstances—and the creative hope of the unknown possible; between the challenge of the present "unity of time" taken as the limiting situation and the challenge of a utopian future; between a consciousness formed by the past historical process and one formed in the creative hope of history.

The dialectical tension is systematized and expressed in the repeated exercises of codifying and de-codifying, through which consciousness is brought into tension with the world around it— the individual becomes aware of himself, of his group and of society; he explores the world around him, becomes conscious of history. Finally, he takes stock of himself as man in the historical world. This confrontation of man with his own self-portrait, with himself, dynamizes the development of self-awareness that sets man in the historical and socializing process.[3] Men come to understand that they live in the world, but are different from the world; that they are in (dialectical) relationship, not just in (non-dialectical) contact with it, in such a way that they are subject to the historical process of the evolution of society.

[3] Man becomes a more profoundly incarnate consciousness, "a conscious being", see P. Freire, "The Adult Literary Process as Cultural Action for Freedom", in *Harvard Educ. Review* (Cambridge, Mass., No. 2, 1970), and *idem*, "Cultural Action and Conscientization", in *ibid.*, No. 3, 1970. In effect, each human being only acquires a critical self-awareness to the extent that he understands himself as existentially and essentially a social and historical being, as a participant in the process of integration of society and dynamization of history: socialization and historicization. The subjectivity-objectivity tension therefore embraces and manifests a whole series of interconnected dialectics: between consciousness and individual, individual and group, group and society. The outward sign of these dialectical tensions is creative activity, which presupposes and conditions a mode of thought: activity and thought constitute practice, which is particularly and characteristically human. Practice is made up of culture, self-expression, communication, the political integration of a society, educational interaction . . . its various aspects make up a practice that, at best, takes the form of dialogue.

4. Consciousness and Problem-seeking Discussion

At some stage in his development, every man forms a consciousness; that is, throughout his life he is becoming himself
and taking on personal characteristics. At first this consciousness
is of an "I" in contrast to "the world"—world being understood
as nature (all that is not the work of man), culture (objects and
facts resulting from human endeavour), and other men (evi-
dently endowed also with an historical and social consciousness
formed in and by the same process as one's own). So the world
is a "not-I" in contrast to one's own consciousness of oneself.

There is therefore a unique dialectical process, in which consciousness becomes "I" and the world "not-I". So the world is
seen as the world through consciousness. Consciousness becomes
"I" in contrast to the world, but also includes a "not-I" com-
ponent, in contra-distinction to all other "I's". The formation of
consciousness therefore depends in practice on historico-social
and existential conditions; that is, on my historical and social
situation, as on that of other people's consciousness. And it is by
virtue of the fact of being a dynamic process of mutual opposition
between two or more poles that the formation of consciousness is
a process in which all the participants are "subjects" and go on
being so without preventing others from playing the role of subject in the process. This relationship between subjects is one of
dialogue.[4] Dialogue is therefore the action of creating a dialectical
process, of making dialectical a relationship that is not so of itself,
of unveiling the dialectics overlaid by myths.

A basic characteristic of consciousness that does not engage in
dialogue is the elimination of problems or the negation of dialectical tension through more or less magical, fatalistic or mechanistic explanations of the universe. Dialogue reveals the problems
inherent in these explanations; it shows them to be doubtful, and

[4] The concept of dialogue includes relationships between equals, critical
approach, dialectical approach, and more, humility, love, cultural synthesis,
co-operation. On this, see P. Freire, *Pedagogy of the Oppressed, op. cit.*,
ch. 4, and *Educação como Práctica da Liberdade, op. cit.*, ch. 1. It does
not exclude what is normally called dialogue: conversation, dealings between people, attention to what the other person is saying. What is being
analysed is a basic approach that any purely verbal dialogue must suppose
and bring out, to the extent that it becomes conscious of being an active
moment in the process by which consciousness is formed critically.

in the final analysis false, because they are alienated or alienating. In doing so, it brings into question the relationships between man and the world, the world and man, the individual and society, society and history, history and humanization. So the instrument of problem-seeking provoked by dialogue is criticism. On finding that its relations with the world are dynamic, and that its own reality is an historical dynamism, consciousness begins to lose its static-fatalistic certainties. What was previously a "magical consciousness", immersed in the world, now becomes one capable of perceiving the "movement of history", comes out in the direction of history and becomes "transitive". As soon as it moves beyond ingenuous and mechanistic explanations of the movement of history, it becomes critical.[5] The magical, the intransitive and ingenuous and the critical consciousness are the three most salient stages in the development of self-awareness, in the process through which consciousness surpasses itself and grows in critical and social analysis and in historicity.

5. *Education for Humanization*

This process also takes on the character of mutual interaction between consciousnesses. Consciousness never comes to the end of the process of self-formation, which also perpetuates the process of differentiating the world from oneself: where there is consciousness, there is a world. Both are in the process of being formed all the time. The basic consequence of this is the possibility of action that will influence other consciousnesses as well as one's own. Such activity can either be educative, to the extent that it brings about conditions that favour the formation of a critical consciousness, or else de-humanizing, to the extent that it impedes certain aspects of the dialectical processes that go to make up liberty—creative capacity, expression, communication. The basic form of interaction between consciousnesses, or of

[5] Ingenuous explanations of the process are those that tend to read history into the present (bourgeois ideas of adaptation), or try to force the present back into the mould of the past, or into that of the future (right and left wing sectarian groups, respectively). The mechanistic concept is one that holds that it is sufficient to change some elements in the historical reality for the whole of it to change "automatically" in a humanizing direction. See, for example, I. Illich, "The Myth of Development", in *I-DOC International*, 1970, pp. 23–39.

mutual development of self-awareness, of the mutual formation of consciousness, is given the name and form of "educative dialogue".

Education is therefore the activation of the process of development of self-awareness, the introduction of a problem-seeking dialogue. It consists in establishing a practice of humanization betweeen one consciousness and another. In this sense education contributes to the process of making man more fully human, since by increasing his capacity for reflection and by exercising his capacity for action and for dialectical relationship, it strengthens his historical position and realization of his vocation as subject of the processes in which he takes part. Education as dialogue is not a matter of implanting knowledge or of imposing attitudes and training people to put them into practice. This would be a "mercenary", "anti-dialogal" education, since it would merely be "depositing" various matters in an inert recipient. Education for humanization is the opposite of this: the exercise of problem-seeking dialogue. By the process of categorizing and de-categorizing, for example, man is continually brought face to face with himself and so with the world and the society he lives in, and is stimulated to activity, expressiveness and communication. Education as dialogue is the dynamizing of dialogue between man and man, between man and the world, between man and the creator: it is putting into practice the fact that "men educate each other, through the medium of the world".

This education tends to bring out an anthropology. It requires a political system that frees man for the free exercise of its practice. Politically, it both supposes and activates a "cultural" revolution, in that it finds the problems inherent in alienating and alienated cultural conditions. In the oppressive societies created by capitalist liberalism and pseudo-socialism, this alienation is built into the political and economic systems that defend privileged minorities against the emergence of the oppressed minorities. This leads to a stunting of creative ability, to repression of communication so that self-awareness either cannot progress any further or is even forced to turn backwards, to the ingenuous and magical stages from which it was emerging.

6. *The Consciousness of the Oppressed*

The oppressed are the main recipients of Freire's educational efforts. The oppressed are those whose actions are limited by others, those whom others try to reduce to the status of object of a particular process. Their consciousness is forcibly held back in the pre-critical stage, or forced to regress even further for the sake of survival. In society, "they have no voice", they can neither express themselves nor create, nor even communicate their needs convincingly. In history, they have had no function: they have been used as beasts of burden, as a machine to produce progress for others, to maintain or restore the privileges of others.

In a welfare state they are the dazzled, massed victims of the mechanics of production and distribution of luxury and consumer goods. They are wooed as recipients of the paternalistic generosity of those who pull the strings of the mass consumption society, who need consumers to keep their production lines moving, and who need an uncritical mass whose tastes can be kept uniform if their production runs are to be kept long enough to push them into high profit areas.

So the oppressed, as described here, are the personification of the idea of the "happy slave". Born and brought up in an atmosphere of oppression, they never have a chance to see reality through their own eyes. Reality for them is patronage and "the goods of this world", and they are no more than a part of this reality; they live for others. This means that their consciousness is not simply an oppressed consciousness, but one that harbours an alien consciousness in itself: their consciousness is host to the consciousness of the oppressor. "The oppressed look at us with the eyes of the oppressors."[6]

[6] The most significant summary of the consciousness of the oppressed is the expression used by Chilean peasants to describe the relations between landowner, foreman and rural worker: "There are men made to work and some made not to work. . . . The first work as best they can, and the others don't." Analysed in P. Freire, "Acción cultural libertadora", interview in *Víspera* (Montevideo, May 1969), pp. 23-9.

Religion, particularly in its "popular" forms, is often one of the main contributory factors in introducing an oppressive mentality, whether through its strong charge of alienation or superstition, or through its support for the *status quo*. It is not easy to summarize the syncretism represented by "Christianity" or even "Catholicism" in Brazil. Tristão de Athayde gives a succinct résumé in his much-admired article, "Cath-

If one sees this situation merely as a primitive stage of economic deprivation, then the obvious remedy is to re-distribute
wealth, so that the poor can stand on their own feet. Then the
oppressed will be an apprentice for the rest of his life: once he sees
himself as the possessor of worldly wealth, he will act like the
boss of the old times, who was always basically his ideal. Then
there is no humanization, either of the oppressed or of the oppressor. Or one could on the contrary make no attempt to re-
structure society or integrate the oppressed in the historical
process, but merely attempt to teach them to throw out the
"parasite" consciousness of the oppressor. Such a course would
have an equally dehumanizing effect. It would be indoctrination
or an attempt to impose an ideology and not a course of develop-

olicism", in *Enciclopédia Delta Larousse*, IV. The writings of Boaventura
Kloppenburg are basic to the question. A more specific and interpretative
attempt is to be found in the sociological essays of the anthropologist
Thales de Azevedo, particularly "O catolicismo no Brasil", in *MEC*, 1955,
which he revised and re-published in "Catolicismo no Brasil?", in *Vozes*,
Feb. 1969 (a special number on the religion of the poor in Brasil), pp. 117–
124. Joseph Comblin supported his analyses in "Os siais dos tempos e a
evangelização", in *Duas cidades* (São Paolo, 1968). See also, Azevedo, "A
sociologia da Religião no Brasil", in *Vozes*, May 1965, pp. 328–33. The
works of Roger Bastide are also indispensable, particularly *Les religions
africaines au Brésil* (Paris, 1960), and *Brésil, terre des contrastes* (Paris,
n.d.). Both works contain valuable bibliographies.
    One can obtain an approximate idea of the situation from a typology
similar to that used by Azevedo in his *Vozes* article. Statistically, more
than 90% of Brazilians call themselves Catholics. Of these the vast majority
practise a "popular" Catholicism, much closer allied to the animism or
fetichism of the original negro slaves than to Christianity, from which it
merely takes Christian names for its "prayers". The correlation between
this form of religion and the poorer classes is obvious, but not exclusive.
A *cultural* or social Catholicism "would show itself in its influence on
institutions, customs and values. *Formal* Catholicism has adequate knowledge of the Catholic faith and its prescribed beliefs, and a desire to practise religion for the sake of giving the impression of being 'good Catholics'
through obvious religious observances. *Nominal* Catholicism shows a per-
functory identification and superficial relationship to the Church, combined with a free interpretation of some of its doctrines" (*Vozes*, Feb.
1969, p. 122). The picture is further complicated by present-day liturgical
and theological movements, not to mention the identification of various
Catholic groups with revolutionary movements, students, "popular culture"
groups, "committed" priests, progressivists, etc. Needless to say, Paulo
Freire and his immediate helpers belong to the "committed" category,
and are tackling "popular" religion.

ment of self-awareness; firstly, because it fails to take into account the fact that consciousness is not formed by forcing concepts into it, but through dialogue with the real situation in which it exists; secondly, because it would be frustrating and would not produce a really valid instrument for the transformation of society.

The effect of education as the simple transmission of knowledge of a written code is not very different—it merely imposes the cultural values of the oppressor on the oppressed. There is also an enormous difference between restructuring the distribution of wealth, with the social and historical integration of the oppressed required by the development of self-awareness and the reform of structures brought about by partial transformations of the historical reality.[7] The historical approach has to be that of making the oppressed aware of their own situation, of stimulating their capacity for dialogue with their situation and with other men, and of seeing the problems inherent in that situation, so that they can re-build the world on the basis of this dialectic, in a continual process of reflection on what they have gone through and on the changes they have brought about. Given that the situation of oppression is a world-wide one, only those who freely renounce the attitude of oppression and identify themselves with the oppressed can be said to cease to be oppressors. Only in this way will they be able to form a more dynamic critical consciousness, one that will be capable of introducing humanizing changes into the world and into itself.

[7] For "revolution" as a means of restructuring the distribution of goods, historical integration and forming a critical consciousness, see P. Freire, "The Adult Literary Process . . .", op. cit., and "Cultural Action and Conscientization", op. cit. Partial transformations of society are necessary and indispensable, but insufficient. The effect of road-building programmes, irrigation schemes and the like is at first to elevate the way of life of certain groups and individuals, a "social advancement". But it runs the risk of remaining at this stage—and dehumanizing—if it is not accompanied by a genuine revolution, which humanizes both oppressors and oppressed.

This observation reflects the self-appraisal made by Paulo Freire and published on the initiative of Linda Bimbi under the title, "The Risks of Conscientization", in I-DOC International, 1–15 Mar. 1972, pp. 22 ff. On page 16 of the same issue there is a most interesting conversation between Freire and Ivan Illich, known for the radicalism of his views and for his admiration of Freire's work. This announces the coming publication of a book in which these subjects will be discussed. See also the works of Francisco Weffort

III. CHRISTIANITY

Historically, the preaching of Christ's message must be said to have had an ambiguous effect on the development of consciousness within society to date, and particularly within groups that have remained at the magical or the intransitive and ingenuous level of thought. The ingenuous consciousness tends to take the preaching of Christianity as an extra-terrestrial explanation, as something outside history, and it has been preached in such a way as to feed magical concepts, to create myths that serve to build up a magical mode of thought, which then becomes a source of alienation with regard to the world. The dialectics historically embodied by Christianity, on the other hand, take on the character of denouncement and announcement—denouncement that brings man face to face with his real situation, that is, with the society in which, historically, he lives; announcement that brings him face to face with his vocation to be the subject of history, the image and likeness of God. Denouncement that opens up the hope of overcoming the factors that are opposed to his liberation; announcement that reveals the progressive, historical working out of the "divine plan of salvation" in this endeavour, and shows that the promises of Christ are the basis of hope. Denouncement is a recognition of the actual limitations of history and announcement is a recognition of the call to go on transcending oneself indefinitely, to be subject to "the image and likeness of the Creator". Denouncement impels men to courageous criticism, to revolution even. Announcement situates and demonstrates the criteria behind this criticism, the basis of this courage, the moving spirit behind and ultimate aim of this revolutionary impulse.[8]

In effect, if being a man means being a subject, not an object, denying man the historical conditions in which he can fulfil this call is a two-edged weapon. On the one hand, it maintains those who are treated as objects in a state of dehumanization and oppression. On the other, it dehumanizes those who claim exclusive exercise of the role of subjects of history, whether in order to per-

---

[8] Denouncement and announcement: see P. Freire, "Tercer mundo y teología", in *Perspectivas de diálogo* (Montevideo, Dec. 1970), and "Carta a un jóven teólogo", in *ibid.*

petuate the present, whose injustice is plain, or to restore the past, as though history were a reversible process, or to anticipate the future, as though the future were capable of being monopolized by human interests.

"The greatest proof of love is therefore to remove the oppressor's possibility to continue oppressing." In the synthetic context sketched out here, this means bringing about a restructuring of the relationships of possession and of historical social integration, in such a way that society will be based on dialogue, not on oppression.[9]

Translated by Paul Burns

[9] V. Schaull, Foreword to *Pedagogy of the Oppressed, op. cit.* Other works to consult: P. Freire, *Extensión o communicación?* (Santiago de Chile, 1969); P. Freire and others, different articles in *Suplemento ISAL* (Montevideo, 1968), called a contribution to the process of conscientization in Latin America, not published commercially; P. Freire, "Politische Alphabetisierung", in *Lutherische Monatshefte* (Berlin/Stuttgart, Nov. 1970), pp. 578–83; P. Freire, *Pädagogik der Unterdückten* (Berlin, 1971); H. Conteris and others, *Conciencia y revolución* (Montevideo, 1969); R. Alves, *A Theology of Human Hope* (Washington, 1969).

Siegfried Schmidt

The "Destruction" of Language in Modern Literature?

1. *"Destruction"?*

NEGATIVE categories seem to be the only conceptual tools with which the increasingly unintelligible developments of "modern" literature can be grasped. According to the value systems and expectations of the critics, such categories are used either dismissively in the context of culture-criticism (H. Seydlmayr) or in an (unsuccessful) attempt at neutral definition. Again, according to the position of the critics, the negative term "destruction" is either given a question-mark or used as a statement of fact.

The title of this article in the form proposed by the editors, that is, without the question-mark, probably embodied the widespread view that, in modern literature, not only have "positive" contents been lost, but that even the medium of this literature, language itself, has been or is being destroyed. Against this claim, Harald Weinrich has suggested that "unhappiness . . . like all forms of evil, untruth and ugliness, in short, negativity . . . seem to offer more favourable conditions for the shaping of language by the writer", that negative subjects have always been characteristic of literature.[1] Weinrich gives this fact a positive interpretation in his third thesis: "The negativity of literature can be seen as a reaction by authors to the cheerfulness of art", which he regards as "an irreducible quality in the role of the public", their fundamental expectation (*op. cit.*, p. 12). The first

[1] H. Weinrich, *Literatur für Leser, Essays und Aufsätze zur Literaturwissenschaft* (Stuttgart, 1971), p. 14.

part of the original view will not be discussed further here, but we shall try in what follows to offer some suggestions for a positive interpretation of the second part, the claim that language is being destroyed

2. *"Experimental" Writing and "Concrete Poetry"*

When "the destruction of language" in modern literature is discussed, the same names usually come up: James Joyce and Gertrude Stein, writers of the futurist and dadaist schools, and E. Gomringer and Helmut Heissenbüttel, as representatives of modern concrete—or as it is dismissively labelled—"experimental" writing. The most dismissive remarks are directed at concrete poetry. "So-called 'concrete poetry', with its machine-made clutter of words and syllables, is too sterile to be worth discussion", according to H. Friedrich,[2] K. Krolow sees here only "dead husks", and P. Rühmkorf speaks of "studies in stuttering and finger exercises on the typewriter". These are obviously extreme positions, and give the sharpest description of the destructive process; they are for that reason important sources for our study. First, however, we shall try to work out some descriptions of the situation and development of literature in the twentieth century which may provide the basis for a discussion of the destruction thesis.

3. *The System of Poetic Communication*

Modern literature, especially poetry, confirms, perhaps more clearly than the literature of any previous period, the hypothesis of many critics since the Russian and Czech formalists that the language of literature is distinguished from other uses of language by specific differences. Generative grammarians, such as R. Levin, have attempted to describe these differences in a theory of deviant style. The main argument in current linguistic studies of literature centres on whether the regularities of the use of language in poetic texts should be combined in an independent poetic grammar, or whether all that is needed is a number of rules for the poetic use of language in addition to the rules of "normal"

[2] H. Friedrich, *Die Struktur der modernen Lyrik* (Hamburg, 9th edn., 1966).

grammar.[3] Whatever the result of this argument, it shows that the poetic use of language seems clearly to follow its own (autonomous) rules which differ from the normal rules, which necessarily implies that the reception of poetic texts must also follow rules of its own which differ from the normal ones. In short, an independent communication system seems to have been developed in the course of history which could be labelled "poetic communication". A characteristic feature of the texts which are received and discussed as "poetic" in this communication system is that the language of the poetic text is not regarded and used merely as a means of conveying information, but is the centre of interest for its own sake, as the language of the text: it is de-instrumentalized, de-functionalized. This process has been described in detail by critics since the nineteen-twenties.[4]

4. Writing becomes "Linguistic"

Among all the diversity of forms, programmes and developments, one point of convergence can be seen in the art of this century, a radical concentration on its media, its means of expression, its "language", which has become a subject in its own right and has pushed other subjects into the background. This process cannot be considered in isolation from the academic and cultural developments of this century which have made discussion in terms of scientific theory and linguistic philosophy of the processes which make up meaning a main preoccupation in all fields. This questioning of all "contents", and of the scope and adequacy of theories of any sort, is now exemplified mainly in a questioning of language.

It is impossible to limit this process to formal problems in epistemology or the logic of science; it is part of a development in which interpersonal communication has become problematic to an extent previously unknown, as a result of doubt of the capacity of language to bring about any adequate, precise and unambiguous expression of thoughts and feelings. The much discussed "language crisis" of the modern writer, which has become a commonplace of twentieth-century literature since Hof-

[3] For details see T. A. van Dijk, *Beiträge zur generativen Poetik* (Munich, 1972): *Grundfragen der Literaturwissenschaft*, vol. 6.
[4] See S. J. Schmidt, *Ästhetische Prozesse* (Cologne, 1971).

mannsthal's letter to Lord Chandos, is a powerful reflection of this situation. Heissenbüttel has written, "It is only a slight exaggeration to say that it is now impossible to write a spontaneous sentence in any branch of literature. Only by bringing the rules of grammar into the light of doubt through reflective observation and disruption can I recover a pleasure in language. The pressure towards unreflected language is great, and nostalgia for it ineradicable, but in practice it is no longer possible."[5] The literature of the period from the end of the Second World War to the present in particular is dominated by texts in which the problems of speaking and writing have themselves become central subjects. In many places the new writing is coming very close to linguistic philosophy, just as, to take a radical example, the visual art of the Art and Language Movement is beginning to become a philosophy of art.

These short and somewhat schematic remarks are intended to bring out the following points. Firstly, poetic communication has always been determined by rules of its own which were autonomous or deviated from a (or "the") norm. One of these rules is that the language of poetic texts oscillates between its function as an information medium and its possible consideration and action as the defunctionalized materiality of language. Secondly, the art of the twentieth century—the century of linguistic philosophy, as it is often called—devotes considerable energy to its language problem, both by questioning its media of expression (for example, by questioning the possibility of concrete art and writing; cf. Schmidt, *op. cit.*) and by making its doubts and despair of self-expression and its difficulties in communicating into subjects in their own right.

5. *Expectation and Negation*

According to J. Levy, the process of the history of literature cannot be understood as a development from Standard A, through B, to C, but as a gradual transition from Standard A to not-A. This means that the rejected norms of a dominant standard remain present and effective in the first versions of the succeeding one, as negated or modified. This hypothesis points to the exist-

---

[5] H. Heissenbüttel, *Über Literatur* (Olten/Freiburg, 1966).

ence of a constant in epistemology and the communication theory which implies that anything offered to perception is categorized according to the rules and criteria which have been developed during the process of perception and knowledge which was successful up to that point. We recognize something in terms of our previously successful "histories" of learning and characterization, which form an interpretative system which defines the individual's horizon of expectations. Anything "new" which appears is first fitted into the familiar sorting and interpretative pattern. Only when this fails is the sorting and interpretative pattern either partially modified or replaced by another. The relation between interpretative pattern and possibility of understanding holds equally for both literary and non-literary texts (and uses of speech in general). Our dealings with texts shape our patterns of experience, and it is within the structure of these patterns that we try to master any new text which appears. Texts are new and innovatory when they shatter our structure of expectations and force us to construct a new one in order to master them. (Distinctions should be made between individual structures of expectation and structures of expectation common to a social group or a whole society.)

One implication of this is that a new text, if it is to be receivable, intelligible, must be to some extent capable of being referred back to old structures, even if only negatively, in the sense that what is negated remains visible.[6] From the point of view of epistemology, this allows us to give a positive interpretation of the predominance of negative categories in the description of modern literature. The "new" is defined as the not-old, as the negation of previous experience and expectation, as destruction; this is the simplest way of understanding it.

After this short discussion of the basis of the situation of modern literature, we shall now try to consider some typical manifestations which are discussed negatively as examples of the "destruction" of language in modern literature.

6. *Ways in which Language becomes a Subject in Modern Writing*

When an author tries, either as a deliberate act or as a spon-

[6] W. Nöth, *Strukturen des Happenings* (Hildesheim, 1971).

taneous reaction, to make language and the problems of expression connected with it the subject of his work, in his text, or as the text itself, there are in theory three procedures open to him, though in practice they are usually found in combination. Firstly, he may try to exhaust all the conceivable forms of language and linguistic expression (including a mixture of languages), even to the extreme of complete unintelligibility. We shall call this "hypertrophy". Secondly, he may adopt the opposite procedure, with silence as its extreme, which rejects the existing modes of speech as intolerable chatter and concentrates on the elements of language. We shall call this procedure "elementarism". Finally, he may try to make the use of language and the structures of the linguistic system into a subject, i.e., he may operate, at least partly, meta-linguistically. We might call this "grammaticalism" ("ism" here is not meant pejoratively). We shall now offer examples of these three possibilities.

7. *Language as Subject in Hypertrophy*

That the reality of a literary text is its language, that it only exists in its language, is true of all literature. That the process of creating a world in and through language can be the only obvious subject of a book was shown in a radical way first by James Joyce in *Finnegans Wake*. After *Dubliners* and *Ulysses*, in which associations in the "internal monologue" already smothered the presentation of objects in description, in *Finnegans Wake* the word emancipates itself completely. It is split up and combined, grows according to phonetic, semantic, etymological, logical and associative, linguistic and musical rules, veers to and fro between no fewer than nineteen languages (from Sanskrit to Old Icelandic) is an attempt to take the world apart in language and build it up again through language. The linguistic and encyclopaedic knowledge of a lifetime's study are massed into a hypertrophied linguistic cosmos, as may be seen from this short example: "Where flash becomes word and silents selfloud. To brace congeners, trebly bounden and asservaged twainly. Adamman, Emhe, Issossianusheen and sometypes Yggely ogs Weib. Uwayoei! So mag this sybilette be our shibboleth that we may syllable her well! Vetus may be occluded behind the mou in Veto but Nova will be nearing as their radient among the

Nereids."[7] Finnegan's fall is accompanied by a word of a hundred letters containing the word "thunder" in languages from Madagascan to Germanic: "bababadalgharaghtakamminarronnkonn-bronntonnerronntuonnthuuntrovarrhounawnskawntoohoohood-enenthurnuk!"

Joyce's method stretches the possibilities of language and the capacity of reception to their limits, but leaves the principle of narrative untouched, although the hypertrophy of symbolisms stretches this also to the limits of reconstruction. Joyce's work is an ultimate point of possible narrative, in which the material, vocalic self-presentation of language and its function as a method of building up a reality coincide as a totalization of language.

8. *Language as Subject in Elementarism*

A quite different way of making language autonomous can be seen in our second method, which can be illustrated by some views and processes from the field of concrete literature, and especially from visual poetry (for further details, see Schmidt, *op. cit.*). According to one of the founders of the concrete movement, E. Gomringer, "silence distinguishes the new writing from individualistic writing. for this purpose it relies on the word. . . . it appropriates for the word the beauty of the material and the adventure of drawing. in certain connections with other words it loses its absolute character. that is what we want to avoid in our writing."

Concrete writing concentrates radically on language as material and meaningful sign, its elements, rules and possibilities of combination. In its manifestation as visual poetry it makes use of writing and therefore incorporates the writing surface as an element of the text. In its manifestation as phonetic poetry it uses language as a source of sound. Language becomes at the same time material, subject and concept. Concrete writing is the first form to abandon completely the principle of narrative which had been retained by all other forms of literature up to the present, and in consequence of this the linear or successive text construction necessary under the old principle was also abandoned and replaced by constellations, montage and collage or the arbitrary

[7] James Joyce, *Finnegans Wake* (New York, 1959), p. 267.

arrangement of material (graphic) linguistic elements. The principle of meaning has been replaced by the principle of "concretization". Concrete texts are what they are. They produce in the first place nothing but themselves, and only this whole complicated process later acquires "meaning" through systems of interpretation which illuminate it. For a proper appreciation of concrete writing it is important to realize that the sparingly used linguistic elements should not be seen as the remnants of a process of reduction; they are rather text-nuclei out of which the recipient can develop text-possibilities, generative nuclei, as it were, elementary rules for the creation of possible texts, which demonstrate the process, the conditions and rules for the formation of meaning in language and texts and bring them into the consciousness of the recipient.

9. *Language as Subject in Grammaticalism*

In this method, which is used in the circle of concrete writing and/or by concrete writers, language becomes a subject. In particular grammatical and syntactic structures are presented and thereby linguistic rules, which otherwise are applied automatically, are made conscious once more. Gertrude Stein is perhaps the earliest example of such writing, as in her text "a rose is a rose...". Helmut Heissenbüttel or the two Czechs, B. Grögerová and J. Hiršal, are modern exponents of the technique. "Simple Grammatical Meditations", "Quantity with Imposed Metre", "Grammatical Reduction" or "Political Grammar" are some of the titles, and indicate the combination of objective linguistic descriptions and meta-linguistic reflection on language. These texts and the most recent attempts at conceptual writing (for example, by H. Gappmayr, J. Gerz, U. Carrega and S. J. Schmidt) announce a development in which the boundaries between types of text could be overcome and theory and practice, science, philosophy and poetry could be integrated.

10. *Constructive Negativity*

Having discussed, too briefly and in insufficient detail,[8] the

[8] Completeness would require taking account of new ways of using language in Italian futurism, German expressionism, Dada and surrealism, which it would be hard to fit into the above schemata.

manifestations and attitude of a treatment of language which appears to many contemporaries as no more than "destruction", we shall return to the question how such a judgment as destruction could ever have been made and how it might be revised.

H. Friedrich, who admits to being no avantgardist and more at home with Goethe than with T. S. Eliot, expresses clearly the discomfort of perhaps most readers of so-called modern literature: "This communicative comfort is just what modern writing refuses to provide. It turns away from humanity in the traditional sense, from "experience", from feeling, sometimes even from the person of the writer. The writer is not involved in his work as a private person, but as a literary intelligence, a linguistic operator.... We can speak of an aggressive conception in modern literature ... it even determines the relation between poem and reader and produces an effect of shock of which the reader is the victim. He does not feel reassured but alarmed" (*op. cit.*, p. 17). Modern writing "deforms reality", literary language "retains the character of an experiment", image and metaphor are clumsily handled, the reader receives "an impression of anomaly", and modern writing remains "unassimilable" (*ibid.*, pp. 16–18). That is the more or less complete catalogue of the objections to modernity. The reason for their appearance, for the critics' concentration on negative categories, is also clear in Friedrich: "The reader also has the right, however, to take his standards from earlier writing and set them as high as possible. We refrain from measuring with such standards, but we permit ourselves to use them as tools for description and recognition" (*ibid.*, p. 19). Friedrich here gives clear confirmation of the hypothesis presented in section 4 of this article: to the system of expectation and interpretation constructed from familiarity with pre-modern literature modern literature appears as ab-normal, as a disappointment of its expectations of narrative language. In this concept we have perhaps a key to the whole phenomenon. The driving force of the development of modern literature is not its anti-traditionalism but its "constructive negativity". This concept allows us to grasp the tendency in modern writing (and modern art in general) to turn the norms, rules, expectations and limits of the process of poetic communication step by step—and in hindsight almost systematically—into subjects, either by questioning and modifying them or by transcending them and replacing them by others. This process has acted on both content and form, and affected the position and function of all the elements involved in the process of poetic communication, author, text, reader, critic, scholar, as well as the understanding of the relation between poetic and non-poetic communication, between art and society. Since Mallarmé all non-archaizing and non-imitative literature has been "experimental" in the sense that it has subjected the whole phenomenon of "poetic communication" and its structure to examination and systematic dissection. The end of art has been a constant theme of poetic communication for over a century, and only an extraordinary fixation on the dream of "communicative comfort" could misunderstand this fundamental process of experiment so as to reduce it to a source of discomfort. In this process there are no longer any hereditary rights, whether the primacy of narrative, imitation or mimesis, the idea of the primacy of the subjective, of metaphor, of symbolic language, of inner meaning or of the general human subject. The claim that seemed so plausible, that what is is, avoided the question why what is should be, what was the purpose of its being, and what it would be like if it were different or instead of itself something else. Modern writing's intense concentration on its necessarily central subject of language is a logical step, logical in the context of the "world" of this century. That this debate has been carried out logically is proved by the final positions we have described above. That the texts which resulted from this process are "destroying" language can only be claimed by someone for whom anything after Goethe is a falling away from a norm. In the "logic" of this writing it is not the writing that is destroying its language; it is rather refusing to work any longer with language which has been destroyed, it is defending itself against the enormous destruction of language in a century of world wars and ideologies, advertising and mass media. Its defence is to take language seriously, syllable by syllable, and to become aware of the fragile dignity of its existence in language and language alone.

Translated by Francis McDonagh

Biographical Notes

ROGÉRIO DE ALMEIDA CUNHA, S.D.B., was born in 1936 in Belo Horizonte, Brazil. A licencié ès lettres néo-latines (Don Bosco Faculty of Philosophy), licencié ès lettres (São João del Rei, Minas Gerais, Brazil), licentiate in theology (Pontifical Salesian Athenaeum, Rome), he has also attended courses on the social doctrine of the Church (Institut Catholique, Paris), French modern literature (Sorbonne), and psychology and pedagogy (São João del Rei). He is now studying for his doctorate in theology under the direction of Professor J. B. Metz at the University of Münster. He is an assistant and a teacher of general sociology and Catholic ethics at the Don Bosco Faculty of Philosophy. He has given lectures and courses in Germany on Paulo Freire and his method.

JERRY GILL studied at the University of Washington, at New York Theological Seminary and at Duke University. Master of arts and doctor of philosophy, he is associate professor of philosophy at Eckerd College (Florida Presbyterian College), St Petersburg, Florida, U.S.A. Among his many published works on religious language are *The Possibility of Religious Knowledge* (1971) and "The Tacit Structure of Religious Knowing" in *Inter. Phil. Quarterly* (January 1970). For a long time he has studied popular culture and radical phenomena.

DANIÈLE HERVIEU-LÉGER was born in 1947 in Paris. A licentiate in law, doctor of sociology, with a diploma from the Institut d'études politiques, Paris, she is assistant lecturer at the Collège Coopératif and at the Institut d'études sociales, Paris. She has done research work in sociology of religion, on the political and religious views of Catholic students in France and on the development of basic communities in a Catholic context. Among her published works are: "De la mission à la protestation" in *L'évolution des étudiants chrétiens en France* (Paris, 1973); "L'Idéologie politico-religieuse des groupes informels d'étudiants: essai d'interprétation" in *Les Groupes Informels dans l'Eglise* (Strasbourg, 1971); "Systèmes de représentations religieuses et politiques dans un groupe d'étudiants catholiques" in *Psychologie Sociale et Religion* (Paris, 1972); "Le développement des communautés de base et leur contexte religieux en France" in *Archives*

Internationales de Sociologie de la Coopération et du Développement, No.
31 (Jan.–June 1972). She has also contributed articles to the reviews *Esprit,
Project, Lumière et Vie, La Maison-Dieu*, etc.

JEAN-PIERRE JOSSUA, O.P., was born in 1930 in Boulogne-sur-Seine and or-
dained in 1962. He studied at the Faculty of Medicine in Paris, at the
Faculty of Theology of the Saulchoir and at the University of Strasbourg.
Doctor of theology, he is professor of dogmatic theology at the Faculties
of the Saulchoir since 1965 and rector of the same Faculties since 1968.
Among his published works are: *La Liturgie après Vatican II* (Paris, 1967:
in collaboration); *Le salut. Incarnation ou mystère pascal?* (Paris, 1968);
Christianisme de masse ou d'élite? (Paris, 1968); and *Que dite-vous du
Christ?* (Paris, 1969: in collaboration).

JEAN MANSIR was born in 1929 in Paris and entered the French Province
of the Dominicans in 1959. He studied at the Faculty of Pharmacy in Paris
and at the Faculties of the Saulchoir. A graduate in pharmacy, licentiate
and reader in theology, he is director of the "Lacordaire Centre" at the
Couvent Saint-Jacques in Paris, assistant lecturer in divers study groups
and organizations, in particular the Interdiocesan Centre of Catechetics in
Paris, and organizer of many sessions on the permanent formation of
priests. His recent articles include "L'inconfort et l'espérance des chrétiens
après le Concile in *Communautés Nouvelles*, 25 (1970) and "Division des
et vérité de l'Eucharistie—et—Communions réalisées ou unité perdue? in
Paroisse et Liturgie, 5 (September 1972).

JOHANN BAPTIST METZ was born in 1928 in Welluck (Germany) and ordained in 1954. He studied at the Universities of Innsbruck and Munich.
Doctor of philosophy and of theology, he is professor of fundamental
theology at the University of Münster. Among his published works are:
Christliche Anthropozentrik (Munich, 1962); *Zur Theologie der Welt*
(1968); *Politische Theologie* (1969); *Befreindes Gedächtnis Jesu Christi*
(1970); and *Die Theologie in der interdisziplinären Forschung* (1971). The
first three books mentioned have been translated into many languages.

EDWARD SCHILLEBEECKX, O.P., was born in 1914 in Antwerp and ordained
in 1941. He studied at the Dominican Faculty of Theology of the Saulchoir, and at the Ecole des Hautes Etudes at the Sorbonne. Doctor of
theology (1951) and master of theology (1959), he has been professor of
dogmatic theology at the University of Nijmegen since 1958 and a visiting
professor at Harvard University; he is also editor-in-chief of *Tijdschrift
voor Theologie*. Among his published works are: *Openbaring en theologie; God en mens; Wereld en Kerk; De zending van der Kerk; Geloofs-
verstaan: Interpretatie et kritiek*; and *God, the Future of Man*.

SIEGFRIED SCHMIDT was born in 1940 in Jülich (Germany). From 1960 to
1965 he studied philosophy, linguistics, germanistics, history and the history of art at Freiburg im B., Göttingen and Münster. Doctor of philosophy, he has been professor of stylistics at the University of Bielefeld
since 1971. Among his published works are *Sprache und Denken als
sprachphilosophisches Problem von Locke bis Wittgenstein* (The Hague,

1968); *Bedeutung und Begriff. Zur Fundiering einer sprachphilosophischen Semantik* (Vol. 3 of the series "Wissenschaftstheorie, Wissenschaft und Philosophie") (Braunschweig, 1969); *Visuelle Poesie, Thesen und Textzyklus, Ava-Manifest 1* (Andernach, 1970); *Ästhetizität. Philosophische Beiträge zu einer Theorie des Ästhetischen* ("Grundfragen der Literaturwissenschaft", Vol. 2) (Munich, 1971); *Ästhetische Prozesse. Beiträge zu einer Theorie der nicht-mimetischen Kunst und Literatur* (Cologne, 1971); and *Zeit—Zyklus* ("Schriften zur konkreten Kunst", Vol. 6) (Karlsruhe, 1971).

ROBERT SPAEMANN was born in 1927 in Berlin. He is professor of philosophy and pedagogy at the Universities of Stuttgart and Salzburg. He has published studies on de Bonald (1959) and Fénelon (1963).

ANDRES TORNOS was born in 1927 in Madrid. He is a doctor of theology (Innsbruck, 1959), doctor of philosophy (Munich, 1960), and holds a diploma in clinical psychology (Madrid, 1964). From 1960 to 1970 he worked especially in the domains of philosophical anthropology and religious psychology. He is professor in the Department of the Sciences of Man and Philosophy at the Pontifical University "Comillas". His recent publications include: *Sociedad y Teología. Essays sobre las condiciones objetivas del pensiamento cristiano* (Bilbao, 1971)) and "El Lenguaje también es Frente de Lucha", article on *Sade, Fourier, Loyola* by R. Barthes, in *Critica* (Madrid, April 1972).

HARALD WEINRICH was born in 1927 in Wismar (Germany). He studied at Münster, Freiburg im B., Toulouse and Madrid. Doctor of philosophy (Münster, 1953), he has been professor at the Universities of Kiel and Cologne, and visiting professor (1963–64) at the University of Michigan. He is now professor at the University of Bielefeld. He is a member of the P.E.N. Club and of the German Academy of Language and Poetry. Among his published works are: *Das Ingenium Don Quijotes* (Münster, 1956); *Phonologische Studien zur romanischen Sprachgeschichte* (Münster, 1964; new completely revised edn. 1971); *Französische Lyrik im 20. Jahrhundert* (Göttingen, 1964); *Linguistik der Lüge* (Heidelberg, 1970[4]); and *Literatur für Leser. Essays und Aufsätze zur Literaturwissenschaft* (Stuttgart, 1971).